Knowing No Boundaries

By
Hannah Daly

Knowing No Boundaries

First published 2022, Dublin, Ireland by Hannah Daly.

For all contact details and more information about this book, the author and disability awareness and inclusion please visit

www.knowingnoboundaries.com

Amazon Print on Demand Edition

ISBN 978-1-7392268-2-4

Knowing No Boundaries

A memoir of my life with dyslexia, dyspraxia and sensory processing disorder.

By

Hannah Daly

A lot is known about dyslexia. The degree to which it affects a person can differ greatly depending on its presentation and severity. Dyslexia can often coexist with other conditions. It can frequently overlap with dyspraxia, a condition that is less well known. Dyspraxia means a disorder of "praxis", a term referring to the ability to plan and carry out movement. Dyspraxia is often simply seen as a deficit in motor co-ordination affecting gross and fine motor skills. People with dyspraxia, however, often experience general issues with sequencing, planning, and execution, alongside regulation of emotions and navigation of social situations. Some manifestations of dyspraxia can be rooted in sensory processing dysfunction, sometimes referred to as "Somatodyspraxia".

Foreword

The higher you build your barriers, the taller I become

-     *Labe Siffre*

I was born in Dublin, Ireland in 1986, where I lived with my parents and four siblings. I spent time living, studying, and working abroad before making my home back in Dublin. I am a mother of four young children and an occupational therapist. I am also profoundly dyslexic, dyspraxic and have sensory processing disorder.

I've never thought of myself as a writer, but I am a storyteller, and I have stories to tell. You may wonder how someone with severe dyslexia and dyspraxia managed to write a book. I dictated these stories, one by one, bit by bit, had them typed up, and listened to them. I then worked with an editor to help me with spelling, structure, and grammar. The typist, readers, and editor all have skills that I don't, and will never possess. Over the years, I have learnt to work with what I've got, and avoid focussing on what I don't have. It was with the right support that I have brought this book to fruition. I hope this book will generate more awareness of dyspraxia and dyslexia. It is important to understand that this memoir is my experience of living with dyslexia and dyspraxia, and I am not speaking for everyone with these conditions.

My book is laid out in a series of vignettes, which illustrate some of the challenges I faced when trying to interact with systems and conventions, and highlight my determination not to be left out of life. Connection with others is a key theme, and some people I came in contact with were significant catalysts in my becoming who I am today.

I have a detailed memory, and I also have a box filled with objects, reports, photographs, and letters. This archive supported the retelling of my story. For the purposes of this book, some details have had to be changed and pseudonyms given to most characters.

I hope the sharing of my life story can give people the confidence to be themselves and embrace difference. I have learnt the freedom of accepting and loving myself just as I am.

*

Sometimes, I have days where everything seems to be part of a domino effect: I call them "My Very Dyspraxic Days". Just picture it: It's 2014; I'm in London. It's morning and my alarm goes off. I have my shower, and put my clothes on which I laid out the night before. I bang into the door as I enter the kitchen. I eat my cereal and some Weetabix drops off the spoon and onto my top, so I have to change. I'm not quite sure what to wear and I pull all my clothes out of my drawer while trying to get organised. In the process, I end up losing my phone underneath the pile of clothes.

My alarm starts to beep, which means that it is time to leave. I constantly set alarms because I am not good at gauging time. I am under pressure knowing that I am late, so I get a bit flustered. I haven't removed the tags from the top yet and they're irritating me. I decide I need to swap tops. I can't tolerate the tightness of the bra straps so I put on a fabric crop top instead. Then I get my bag and go.

The tube is crowded. I am standing at the tube door waiting to get in and am frantically trying to scan for a free seat – a bit like musical chairs. As soon as the door opens, it is like the music has stopped, and I have to jump in and find a place. Luckily, I get a seat, but the guy sitting beside me has large elbows which are poking into me over the seats' midline (boundaries are very important). The person to my left is blasting

music through their earphones; I can hear *"DOUF DOUF …
DOUF DOUF."* There are really strong smells, and my stress
levels rise.

I am not into music, but one way that I deal with this
sensory overload is with the little MP3 player that my brother got
me. I put it on and listen to whatever's playing, trying to stay
focused.

Finally, I see my stop and get off the tube. I feel fizzy
inside. I have planned to meet a friend for hot chocolate. Because
of the head space that I am in, I decide to play it safe and get a
bottle of water to take away. If they had made the hot chocolate
wrong, I know that it would tip me over the edge! Some days I
can cope with being in a busy environment: if I haven't been late;
if I haven't been pushed; if people haven't been in my space; if I
hadn't whacked myself on the doorframe; or if I hadn't spilled my
breakfast … This is not one of those days.

On these Very Dyspraxic Days, more than others, it just
feels like my visual focus is off-line. Everything is slightly crooked
internally, and I don't feel safe externally. I just feel vulnerable.

Chapter One: Early childhood

This too shall pass.

-     *Anon.*

This chapter captures who I was in my early years, and how I chased an education. I have very mixed feelings towards this time in my life, and you'll see why. These years are considered a child's formative years and set the foundation for the person they are to become. My expectations were influenced heavily by fairy tales, and then later movies, but my understanding of myself and my image of what life should be never quite measured up with each other. It is in this period that I felt like the "ugly duckling". My diagnoses helped me realise that I was a swan, or, in my case, something not so graceful.

There is a photograph of me as a toddler in a white, cotton romper, standing on my own in the doorway, in our first family home in Cedarwood Close, Dublin. The photograph was taken shortly after I had started walking. I looked like such a typical toddler, but Mum remembered worrying that I wasn't going to walk. I did not and would not crawl, and showed no signs of pre-walking skills. Then, one day, out of nowhere, I began to walk. I had reached this developmental milestone within the "expected" age range, but I still could not crawl. Now that I was on my feet, there was no stopping me. I would be everywhere at once, banging into anything and anyone.

When I was three I had my first major collision and split my head open for the first time. It was Halloween night. I was taken to the hospital where the doctor just superglued it back together. I escaped with only a small scar on the left side of my forehead.

The following year my family moved house from Cedarwood Close to a small bungalow in need of love and repair in the countryside in north County Dublin. At the time, the family car was an old black Morris Minor which was parked on the long, stony driveway leading up to the bungalow. My big brother, Stuart, was seven and a half, my big sister, Ruth, was six, and my little brother, Robert, was one and a half at the time. One evening, Mum was in the house with Robert, while Stuart, Ruth, and I were playing in the garden. Mum called us in for supper. Ruth said, "Let's race!" which Stuart countered with, "Last one into the house is a rotten egg!" The stakes were high, and we all began to run our fastest towards the bungalow. And then it just happened, that moment that continues to happen – that moment where I am up and suddenly I am down. I fell. I had been going full force with arms and legs in all directions, and though there was nothing in my way, I suddenly lost my balance and went head first, smacking onto a patio slab. I found myself sliding face down off the edge of the patio onto the bed of pebbles that lined the driveway. Panicked, and unsure what had happened, I began to shriek.

At my cries, Stuart and Ruth ran to me. Stuart asked "Are you okay? What's wrong, Hannah?" I was still face down and not really moving. Roars and screams came from me.

Mum was now outside, standing above me, saying, "Come on, Hannah, get up!" – a tactic she would often use when one of us fell and it wasn't serious. Although this approach was an effective way of teaching us to self-soothe and normalise small blows, this occasion was different. At Mum's words, Stuart and Ruth helped me to sit up, revealing a red-streaked face and blood spurting from a forehead caked with driveway pebbles. The severity of my fall was clear.

Mum, being her assertive self, quickly formulated a plan of action. She dropped off Robert, Ruth, and Stuart at a new neighbour's house, and another new neighbour drove Mum and me, still holding a cloth to my head and crying in the back of the car, to Temple Street Children's Hospital.

Although this was not the first time I had split my head open, this was a more serious fall. On this occasion, the split was just too big for the superglue and my head needed to be stitched back together. I was given a large plaster with a pink elephant and blue mouse on it to stick on my forehead to cover up the stitches. For being so brave, I got to be a nurse and gave my favourite doll, Jenny, a matching plaster for her forehead. I still have the photograph of the two of us with our plasters on our foreheads in my childhood photograph album.

*

One of my earliest memories is from when I was about three, and we were in our first family house in Cedarwood Close. I was downstairs, in the kitchen, standing by the patio doors which led into the backyard. Ruth was already out in the garden, but Stuart was standing by the patio doors, getting his shoes on. We were all going out to play together in the garden, but first I needed to put my shoes and socks on too. I was starting to get a sense of being itchy and uncomfortable. Mum was helping me to put my sock on, but the sock was really hurting me. I told her it was the wrong sock for the foot; I believed socks were like shoes, and had a set side. She then swapped the sock, and began to put it on the opposite – correct – side. The fabric brushed past my toenails, then the seam didn't line up correctly, and I was experiencing pain! I could take no more, and I just lost it. It was so intense, and I became so distressed, that every item of clothing I had on me needed to come off immediately.

I was lying on my stomach, rolling around and crying as I flung every item of clothing from my body. All I wanted to do was go outside, but I couldn't cope with the fact that the sock was touching me. Mum said I didn't like socks that had patterns on them because they had scratchy threads, and I would complain to her that I could feel them. Some people would describe me as being "fussy" or "dramatic", but then one day I declared that I was just like the princess in *The Princess and the Pea*. This was how I experienced – and still experience – these tactile sensations. It is as if there are hundreds of mattresses and only a real princess can feel that there is a pea underneath; I have a great sensitivity to touch, and, as an occupational therapist, I can now recognise this as tactile sensitivity.

*

Rules have always been important to me. One day in playschool, I was throwing a full-on temper tantrum. I was hitting the floor, distressed over the fact that a girl in the class had stolen another boy's crayons. I just could not cope with this; I screamed, "It's wrong! It's not okay to steal the boy's crayons!"

The teacher said, "Hannah, don't worry – we have more."

"That's not the point," I said. "She shouldn't be stealing the crayons. It's against the rules!"

By this point, the boy and girl were now playing happily together, yet I was still distressed by the event, and required support from the teacher to calm myself. Situations and reactions to things like that were regular occurrences for me.

*

On my first day in primary school, I wore a massive oversized uniform. This wasn't an economical purchase, but because I refused to wear a smaller size. I didn't like fitted things. It was a Gaelscoil (an Irish-language school) in County Meath, so everyone spoke Irish, and the teacher's name was Muinteoir.

I didn't really like the classroom environment: it was quite noisy; there were lots of kids; everybody had just begun at the same time; and everyone was the same age. The teacher, Muinteoir, came over to my mum and me to welcome us. When she went to take my hand to take me to my desk, I became anxious and started to cry. I kicked her – a big kick. The sensation of kicking felt good. It gave me calming and grounding feedback. But I felt bad that I had hurt Muinteoir, as that was not my intention. Mum left me to get on with it, and it wasn't long before my tears had stopped and I was a good, cooperative child, settling in.

I sat beside Muinteoir's son, as I liked him the most. He was not like some of the other boys in my class; he was clean and didn't have a snotty nose. He was consistent, dependable, and sensitive, and he became my friend.

In my first year of school, for English lessons, we read a set of books about a girl and boy called *Ann and Barry*. They are very simple books: "Ann went to the shop" and "Barry has a cat." I had a good memory, and learned all of these stories off-by-heart. I could recite them in sequence to the pages, as they had pictures of the story. I would hear the story once or twice, and I would remember it, no problem. I think I had fooled everybody: nobody suspected that I wasn't reading. When I tried to read, I would make up the words, or see the first letter and try to deduce what it might be. It was only when the *Ann and Barry* books became more complicated that this was picked up.

I would say the alphabet backwards, which was unusual; Mum said that I would come out with "Z, Y, X" all the way to "A". I couldn't say it forwards properly at that stage, but I could recite it perfectly backwards.

When asked to read a book that I didn't know, I would simply make it up, using the pictures as a guide. Mum would say to me, "Hannah, that's great, but will you read what's on the page?"

I would reply, "I *would* read what's on the page, if it would sit still. It keeps running around and I can't. I can't read what's on the page."

Mum would ask me if there was anything I could do to stop words from moving around the page. I would tell her that sometimes I could, but "I have to go into my tunnel, Mum. I have to go into my tunnel to be able to read."

The district nurse was due to come to the school to screen all of the children. Part of the parental consent and screening form included a section for any concerns. My mum wrote, *"Eyesight and flat feet?"*, as I was still losing my balance, falling, dropping stuff, and banging into things regularly. Mum thought it must be a problem with my sight; why else would I not be able to see that there was a door in my way, or a chair, or a step?

It was during that visit that I was screened by a district nurse and then a physiotherapist, who asked me to walk a line on the floor like a tightrope, and catch and throw a ball. Following these games, they told Mum that I had a thing called "dyspraxia". She was told that dyspraxia meant that a child had difficulty with balance and gross motor tasks. I had flat feet, but my eyesight was fine. It was my dyspraxia that was causing the difficulties with my balance and accidents.

Mum didn't know much about dyspraxia. This was pre-Google and dyspraxia wasn't well understood. She read the limited available material, which basically said that it was a gross motor difficulty and if a child did horse riding and swimming, they would learn to grow out of it. That was about as much as was commonly known back then. There was no mention of my fine motor skills or handwriting, and the other difficulties that would accompany my new diagnosis.

*

When we were young, we had two Jack Russells: one was called Jessie, and the other one was Daisy. Daisy was my dog, and Jessie was Ruth's. Jessie was a thoroughbred who thought she was a cat and would climb trees. My parents decided to breed Jessie, and had booked to take her to a stud farm. Mum has always been very open with us children, so she decided to inform us about what was going to happen and where Jessie was going. I had lots of questions, to which I was given lots of answers. As a child, I was never very good at keeping secrets or knowing what information was appropriate to share and what wasn't. I just didn't have that ability. I had an aunt who didn't have any children at the time that Jessie had her litter. My aunt had a husband, and I was quite concerned – I couldn't understand why she had no children. Perhaps she didn't know about this business? My aunt was a hairdresser and sometimes saw clients at home. One day, I was over at her house while an elderly client was having their hair done in my aunt's kitchen.

I said, "Auntie, do you know where babies come from?"

She said, "Oh, no, I don't. Don't be asking me that. I have no idea."

"Oh, great!" I replied. "Well, wait until I tell you!" I started explaining the process – probably quite graphically – and the results of Jessie's successful trip to the stud farm. At that, my aunt tried to hurry me out of the kitchen and distract me, stopping me mid-sentence as the elderly client sat in her curlers with an expression of shock and disbelief.

Thereafter, Mum made a point of informing me of anything that wasn't to be shared with everybody; these were now called "secrets". We had lots of secrets in my house, or so I thought.

*

Mum was pregnant with another baby. One morning, when I woke up, a girl who lived up the road was minding us. She told me that Mum had gone into hospital to have the baby. I didn't believe her, and I began searching the house. I pulled back the shower curtain, but Mum wasn't there. We had peach-coloured towels and one large bath-towel was hanging on a rack in our bathroom. I lifted it up, thinking Mum might have been hiding underneath, but she was definitely not there. The babysitter had been telling the truth. Later that day, when we came home from school, Dad drove the four of us into Holles Street Maternity Hospital to meet the new baby. We all gathered around Mum, sitting on her bed. It was a boy; I had another brother, and his name was Killian. He was so tiny and perfect. He also had a thing called Down syndrome and he was deaf. Our family was now complete, and I had officially become the middle child!

That summer, Dad got a wine vat, and he lined it with plastic. We filled it with water and used it as a swimming pool. We put a ladder against the edge so we could climb in. We had little grassy mounds in the garden and we used the left-over plastic sheets to make a slide, squirting fairy liquid on it, and throwing buckets of water on top. Dad also used old tyres to make swings, tying them around tall tree branches with ropes. I would spend hours on my tummy on these tyre swings. With my siblings, we would put a big pile of leaves between two swings. We created a game, which we called the "Gladiator Challenge", where we had to swing on our tummies and gather the most leaves in the shortest time, but without letting our feet touch the ground. We would use our hands to propel ourselves off the ground. I also would climb the tree, place the tyre around my body, and jump. I loved these games and could cope with being dirty, particularly when pushing through my hands and experiencing the sensation of swinging. As soon as I stopped swinging, I needed to get clean immediately because the sensation of the dirt in my nails and on my hands became intolerable.

*

I had very set ideas about what I wanted to be when I grew up. I used to love watching Shirley Temple films, and I would sit and copy her expressions, putting my hand on my hips and furrowing my brow.

My mum came into the bedroom once when I was about two and a half, and I was crying my eyes out standing in front of the mirror.

"Hannah," Mum said, "what's the matter? What happened?"

I wiped my tears away, turned to her with a big smile, and announced, "I'm just practising for the movies, Mum." I was going to be an actress when I grew up.

One long weekend, my cousin and her friend were minding us. My parents had gone away on a holiday. My cousin was 16. I was in the bath for ages, so she came to investigate. We used to have this bottle-green shower curtain, and I would pull it forwards and backwards, and forwards and backwards. I was caught doing this when my cousin came in.

"Hannah, what are you doing?" she asked. "Is everything okay?"

I informed her that she was in my theatre, this was my stage, and "I'm just singing for the boys!"

"What are you doing to the curtains?" she said.

"It is my curtain call, and time for my bow!"

Indeed, the bathroom was my theatre. Often, as a child, I could be found standing by the toilet, and making up a dialogue or singing to the mirror, a performance which was always followed by a flush of the toilet. Mum once asked me why I did this, and I informed her that the toilet flush was my round of applause where I would practise taking my bow. Long before I began drama classes, I had always geared myself towards the arts.

For me, drama was something that was positive because it was something that allowed me to explore and take on new roles, and make believe. It helped me be a bit more flexible in my thinking and interactions from a young age.

Indeed, my future plans were always ambitious. I had wanted to be Mary President. In Ireland at that time, the first female president has been elected, and her name was Mary Robinson. Mum told me that I couldn't be Mary President, but I could be Hannah President. I was very upset about this, because I wanted to be *Mary* President, just like Mary President. Ironically, the next president who came along and took over from Mary Robinson was also called Mary: Mary McAleese. So I was convinced that I needed to change my name to Mary to fulfil this aspiration!

Not being a Mary, I decided to consider other future roles. In Ireland, there is a competition called the Rose of Tralee. It is aired on RTE 1 television for two nights every summer in August (RTE 1 was one of the two television stations we actually had access to growing up!). Girls from all over the world who have an Irish connection come onstage in the Dome in Kerry wearing a ball gown. These girls are known as Roses, and they are ambassadors who tell stories about themselves. I would watch them wearing the most beautiful ball gowns and going on a once-in-a-lifetime trip around Ireland, where they were treated like royalty. Without having a crown of my own, I would put a doily on my head and go around waving, and declaring, "I'm the Rose of Tralee!"

Whenever other children and friends were over, I would cast them as various parts in my plays, and generally most were willing participants. My neighbour would say that I was like the Pied Piper when it came to children; I could just command and engage children, as long as they were younger than me. I could have them all collaborate, moving and working together to create something. I was very entrepreneurial: I always charged the parents to see the plays that I had produced and directed, having them all pay 20p to come into the living room and see the show.

As a child, I shared a bedroom with Ruth. Although she is only two years older than me, I had a set idea of how an older sister should be. I constantly needed Ruth's approval and for her to play a certain role for me. I would find it difficult to go to sleep at night, and my mind would ramble. I loved to chat as it was my way of processing things and communicating. At night, the last thing I would say to Ruth would have to be "Good night, Ruth, love you," and she needed to say, "Good night, Hannah. Love you," and only then could I sleep. But on the occasions that I thought of anything else, or remembered something, I would have to talk again, and then needed to repeat our "Good night, I love you" routine in order to settle. I would always say my part, but Ruth would not always say "I love you" back to me. I regularly got upset about this. I recall one night when I couldn't settle, and couldn't cope with Ruth refusing to engage with me. I ran into the sitting room in tears, saying, "Mum! Ruth won't tell me she loves me!" Ruth still remembers this, and we can laugh about it now. But, as a child, I took this really personally. I guess I was always trying to seek approval from others to feel like I belonged, like I was good enough.

*

I couldn't cope very well with wearing clothes, especially fitted clothes, and I was constantly stripping. If I had any opportunity, I would be naked. I remember one occasion where we were driving with Dad and he pulled the car into a halting site which had many mobile homes, vehicles, caravans, and animals in the yard. Dad told us kids that we had to stay in the car, and he got out and began talking to a man. I asked Ruth and Stuart what was going on; what were we doing here? Ruth informed me that Dad was bringing me back to my real family, as I was adopted and came from this camp. I thought that this made sense, because I was so different from my brothers and sister. I said, "Who is my real family, then?"

They said, "Oh, you are adopted from a nudist colony!" and burst out laughing. At that, I looked out the window at Dad, who was now beside a car looking at spare parts to buy.

There was a strong sense in me of not feeling the same as everyone else, and thinking that I was different, but not fully understanding where this sense of differentness came from.

There is a photograph that shows me at a birthday party: I am the one wearing the large, oversized underwear and nothing else. Everyone else is in their party frocks, and we are all eating birthday cake. This is "classic Hannah". I often wore very baggy clothes. I had to cut every tag off of every top, and not even a little bit could remain because it would scratch me. I had a lovely woollen jumper that I adored, but I could never wear it because it made me itchy. I loved princess-style, flowing dresses because they were baggy. You could twirl in them, and they were comfortable. I adored walking around without clothes on. Even as an adult, I often struggle with wearing fitted clothes. It is a mixture of not wanting to wear restrictive things, and feeling more comfortable in flowy, roomy garments, as well as a reduced ability to gauge if something actually fits me. I often end up buying a size too big for me; even with shoes, I never know if they fit and often rely on others' feedback to help me. As a child, if I tried to tune into whether something fitted, I would get too much feedback think it was too tight, would get distressed, and not be able to make a decision. Therefore it was always safer to go with the bigger size.

When I was younger, I would love walking around barefoot, especially on stony surfaces or grass. I would also love the feel of sponges in my mouth, especially natural sponges. I loved dipping the sponge in the water to make it swell up, and then would put it in my mouth and squeeze the water out. I also loved putting clothes pegs on my eyebrows. The sensation relaxed me and helped me to feel calm. Now, understanding more about sensory processing, I understand that my walking on stones, putting sponges in my mouth, and pegs on my eyebrows were all strategies I developed to help me relax.

There was a particular St Patrick's Day that started like most normal St Patrick's Days. We would wear our Aran jumpers with a handful of clovers safety-pinned on them and go into what we called "town" (Dublin city centre). We'd park in Uncle Tom's car park; Uncle Tom is my great-grand uncle, who used to live in Dominic's Street in the old flats that were there. This was very close to the Ilac Centre and O'Connell Street, as the parade always went past O'Connell Street. We made our way to the barriers in O'Connell Street and found a spot to watch the parade. I loved the parade, especially all of the street performers. It looked like so much fun, and I wished I could perform with them.

As the parade came to a halt, we made our way back to the car through the Ilac Centre, where we picked up some mint-flavoured green milkshakes that were out especially for St Patrick's Day. It was such a sunny day that Mum and Dad decided we would drive the hour to Brittas Bay Beach. It must have been exceptionally warm weather, because, generally, St Patrick's Day is absolutely freezing.

We got to the beach, parked the car, and walked through the dunes down to the sand. My brothers and sister ran around on the sand, but the water was inviting me in. I stripped down to my undies and got into the sea on my own at first, but was shortly followed by some of my siblings. We had a lovely time, but it was freezing afterwards and we jumped back into the car. We didn't have towels, so we put on our Aran jumpers and trousers, and left the wet undies in the boot.

Dad got some chips in Enniskerry on the way home, which we had to share between all of us siblings in the back seats, and Mum and Dad had some in the front. At the very back of the driver's seat was a little net pouch where Mum used to keep a hairbrush and a few newspapers. Suddenly, an argument broke out; I was wriggling and getting into my sibling's space. I could feel the sand rubbing against my skin. I wasn't wearing any underwear, the Aran jumper was itchy, and the legs of my trousers were damp and sticky. I was becoming overwhelmed by these sensations.

Mum said, "Shh! Settle down, stop fighting!"

Ruth and Stuart were immediately quiet and well behaved, but I continued to move and complain. Mum took the hairbrush from the back of the seat and used it as an extension to give me a poke to tell me to sit still. This was a familiar thing Mum would do when there was messing in the back and she wasn't able to get back to us; it was a serious warning. I had a way of always being the one who got caught.

*

I was brilliant at coming up with ideas and had a great imagination, but I found it difficult to execute them. I might have had a great idea about how to make a poster, but my handwriting would be really squiggly, or I wouldn't spell the words properly, or it wouldn't be symmetrical; it certainly never looked the way I intended it to. There were other kids who would regularly copy my ideas and take credit for them, as they possessed the ability to execute things so much better than me. This frustrated and upset me. I thought about things deeply from all perspectives, and my ideas were often creative and original, but I struggled with making things as polished as others and I often only got criticism for my attempts. One day, I challenged a friend, saying, "This was my idea!", and she said, "Oh, my mum says it's okay to copy other people's ideas." She would claim the idea was her own and get credit for it, which really frustrated me.

Another girl in my class had a great influence on me from the very beginning. When I went to her house for the first time, her dad took us with him to the shops after dinner and told us that he was going to buy us ice creams. I was just going to have an ice-pop, which is what I would usually pick. With a disapproving look, the girl said, "Oh, no. Pick a posh one", and selected a choc ice. Keen to please, I followed suit. No sooner had I bitten into it than I felt disappointed. I would have much preferred my ice-pop. But this girl seemed quite exciting: she knew all about sophisticated things. On one occasion when we had a playdate, her parents took us to an outdoor event. We went to a pub on the way for lunch, and in anticipation, my mum had given me a few pounds in case I wanted to buy a treat for us. I had ordered chips, and again I received that familiar disapproving look because I didn't select the prawn cocktail. We went into the toilet, which had a vending machine with pictures of fruit on it, dispensing what I thought were fruit pastilles for two pounds, which I could get for us all to eat. I was taking two-pound coins out of my bag when she laughed at me and said, "Oh, Hannah, they're condoms."

So I said, "Do they not taste nice?", and then she started to explain to me that condoms were what adults use to have sex.

I was quite disturbed by this – my dog Jessie hadn't needed these – but I did not put my money in to find out, just in case.

As a child I was very impressionable, but I wore my heart on my sleeve and was overly honest. I was so keen to try and keep friends. I put a lot of effort into trying to conform but I struggled to truly fit in.

*

I loved the Gaelscoil, but I was struggling to keep up. The class size was large and they didn't have resource classes. It was felt that a move to a small English-speaking National School would give me a better opportunity without the complexity of learning through Irish. Stuart and Ruth were well settled in the Gaelscoil, so, at aged seven, I moved to a rural, two classroom local school, for second class. Robert started in Junior Infants and was in the same room as me. Our new teacher was so lovely. The class sizes were small and I had access to resource teaching. In theory, this was an ideal move. This certainly was the case until third class.

In third class, I moved into the senior room, taught by 'The Teacher'. The senior class was made up of third to sixth classes combined. I was one of the youngest in the room. I was sitting at an old two-seater classroom desk. I had a pencil in my hand and was leaning so hard on it that it snapped. I went up to the top desk where The Teacher had an electric pencil sharpener. I felt that The Teacher was always criticising and scolding me, implying that I was breaking the pencils on purpose. On this day, I had just sharpened my pencil at The Teacher's table, and walked back to my desk. With my left hand holding my copy book in place, and trying to hold my pencil really tightly in my right, I attempted to write on the page. I overshot the intended line because of the excessive force I was applying through the pencil. The pencil slipped and the lead ended up piercing the little finger on my left hand. My finger began to bleed and the pencil was now in need of re-sharpening. I just sat there, as I was too afraid to go up to The Teacher's desk, in case I was in trouble for having to re-pare my pencil. Instead, I sat looking at my copy book with a broken pencil and blood dripping from my finger. This injury was to scar, and leave me with a permanent reminder of my handwriting skills.

I was always very good at maths, especially with numbers; numbers made more sense than letters. We had begun to do mathematical word problems, like "Johnny has three litres of milk and Mary has four. How many litres do they have between them?" I had difficulty with these types of sums because I was unable to read them, and the numbers were written in English rather than as numerals.

One day, I was getting so frustrated, sitting and looking at this piece of paper with my mind completely blank and unable to connect or understand what was on the page, when I had an idea: I would get someone to read it for me. I put the maths workbook up my jumper and pretended I was going out to the toilets, which were located outside of the classroom. Instead, I ran into the secretaries' office, where I pulled out the workbook and I asked the friendly school secretary to read the questions to me. She read four questions, and then told me that I must get back to class. I shoved the book back under my baggy jumper and returned to my desk where I then began solving the maths problems. I could now do them, as I had converted them into numeral sums.

Later that day, after I had handed in my maths workbook, The Teacher called me up to the top of the class and asked me if I had copied from someone else as I usually got these type of sums wrong. I felt so upset and disempowered. Prior to this, I would often ask The Teacher to read the questions out loud. The Teacher would typically respond that they were too busy working with the other classes and to read them myself. Other times, I would sit and not finish my work in time, or just make a guess at the numbers which the letters potentially could be. I would often find that if I got bored and was not able to engage in my work, I would get antsy and agitated, and would move around a lot in my seat. And then I would be accused of being disruptive.

*

Every year there was a Credit Union quiz sponsored by the Cadbury's Chocolate Company. Every school in the area was allowed to send two teams, each comprised of four children and a substitute. The prizes were chocolate, and during the day of the competition, the tables had chocolate in the middle for the quiz teams to enjoy. In our school, The Teacher said that we would have a class quiz to select the teams to represent the school. The Teacher read some questions aloud, and we would have to put our hands up to answer. The top ten people who had answered the most questions would represent the school. I had answered a lot of questions correctly and was in the top 10. I was so excited and was really looking forward to being part of the quiz team, especially as I was getting lots of red marks and "X"s on my schoolwork. That afternoon, though, I was told by The

Teacher that, although I was in the top 10, I was not going to be attending the quiz as you needed to be able to read and write to be on the team. I went home, devastated. I told Mum that it wasn't right and that The Teacher had changed the rules (at that stage I was still very much a "rule police" person).

The next day, I went to school determined to fight for my place. I went to The Teacher's desk first thing in the morning, just before class. I said that I didn't think their decision regarding my place on the team was fair, and that I would still be useful even though I couldn't read and write and that I would like to be on the team. I was told that this would not be possible and that my place had already given away and how would my "friend" feel if I were to go instead of her? I felt conflicted; why did everybody else's feelings matter more than mine? I exclaimed, "It's not about her! It's about *me*! I earned *my* place!"

Needless to say, I did not get to attend the Credit Union Quiz.

*

Due to my difficulties with reading and writing, I was on the school's waiting list to be assessed by an educational psychologist. The waiting lists were long, and my parents did not have the means to fund a private assessment. In the meantime, my mother was proactive in supporting me at home with my schoolwork. When my name eventually came to the top of the list to see the educational psychologist, a letter arrived and we marked the date in the calendar. Dad arranged a day off work, and I got a day off school. On the day of our first appointment, Dad, Mum, and I drove into "town" to the Mater Hospital. I had never been to this hospital before. It was surrounded by high fences, and there was no parking by the entrance. Dad dropped off Mum and me at the door and went to park. I became a little bit concerned because I had only been to hospitals when I had had falls or had been physically sick, but this time I wasn't.

I waited anxiously for a doctor to appear, but instead a lovely lady called Anne, the psychologist, arrived. She immediately engaged with me and brought me to her office, and it did not take long before I was at ease. In her room we played lots of different games from her box of toys and from her workbooks. I had several appointments with Anne. She would ask me questions like, "If you found a letter in an envelope on the floor, and it had a stamp and address on it, what would you do?" to which I responded, "Oh, I would post it." I was asked to read pieces of paper and answer questions on them – comprehension stuff. On my last visit, Anne gave me some stickers and told me I was a very bright girl, and that she enjoyed working with me.

Anne subsequently wrote a report to say that I was profoundly dyslexic, and made recommendations to support me in my education. Mum brought my report in to The Teacher, who dismissed it and went on to say that there was nothing wrong with me; that I was just slow, and they should not put so much pressure on me.

Mum and Dad had a follow up appointment with Anne (without me) after she had completed the assessments in order to discuss my diagnosis. Mum looked for advice, saying, "We have been trying to support her with reading and writing; we have been giving her remedial work; she has been going to the remedial group but she is still struggling. What more can we do to help Hannah with her difficulties?" Anne gave my mum an intensive reading and spelling programme to do at home and strongly suggested that I attend a special reading school called Catherine McAuley's.

Anne also warned Mum and Dad that, as the education system was failing me, and because I was quite a bright child, it was vital that I received the correct support in order to prevent me from making bad life choices or opting out of life. Interestingly, I only learned of this conversation as an adult, but as a nine-year-old, I had in fact already begun to "opt out" as a means to limit opportunities for failure. Anne proceeded to explain that, because I was intelligent and resourceful, it was likely that I would look for alternative opportunities to succeed and fit in, such as getting involved in drugs or crime. Although that may seem a bit extreme, it makes sense, because people make bad choices and reject society when they don't feel like they can be part of it.

I didn't realise at the time that Mum was having those disagreements and discussions with The Teacher about my "ability" and value, the discounting of the report and the belief that I just had a low IQ. However, I felt the negative impact of the comments on my reading and the attitude towards me. I don't know if The Teacher even took the time to read the report, which clearly stated that my diagnosis had been determined through standardised testing, and which confirmed I had an above-average to high IQ. Mum was very disappointed and concerned at this stage, as we had finally been given a name and a reason for my difficulties, but this diagnosis was being dismissed and belittled. I was coming home with classwork not completed and gaps in all my books. Mum tried to highlight this to The Teacher and said that I needed more support. The Teacher responded by questioning why I could do maths some of the time but not others. Mum explained that this was due to my reading issues and the impact that this had on my ability to understand the questions, but this explanation was discounted by The Teacher as the maths problems were written in "simple English",

Mum decided to spend time teaching me and filling in the gaps in my workbooks. This meant that we had to do an extra two hours most nights just for me to keep up with classwork. I was a bright little girl, but I was slipping behind academically.

*

There were a handful of other girls in the class, some of whom were a few years older than me. I remember one day when I walked into the room, an older girl put her foot out to trip me up. She sat in the desk at the front of the class. A small group of my older classmates laughed when I fell. The teacher came back into the room and took the "Roll" in the large book used to check attendance, a process that seemed to occupy so much time.

The Teacher told us all to sit down and take out our readers, and then instructed different children to read out loud. I was picked to read again. It seemed to be the only thing I was picked for. I started to read, but it was difficult. The words moved about, so I tried my best. I'd stutter, then I'd guess. At this stage, The Teacher had started encouraging the other students to correct me when I made mistakes. This had been going on for months. I dreaded being asked to read. An older boy turned around, sticking his tongue behind his bottom lip and making a "duhhh" noise. He would often do this when I really struggled to read a word. I wanted to not exist. I began to panic and got even more words wrong. More people corrected me. I asked "Can I please stop now?", but was informed that I would be told when it was time to stop, so I continued to try. I remember that The Teacher often added an extra element to this "game", as I felt the class had now come to see it. The class now voted on everything: hands up who thought "x" was the best reader, "y" had the best ideas, "z" was the smartest. I felt like I was an animal being played with for everyone else's amusement.

On another day, I remember an older girl decided to stick the sharp point of a geometry compass into my back, through my top. I wanted to cry, but when I tried to tell The Teacher, I was reprimanded for "telling tales" and disturbing the lesson.

On another occasion, I remember The Teacher stood at the doorway talking to the lovely resource teacher who visited the school once a week. I'd come to see my resource time as heaven. The resource room was small and the sun always seemed to shine on the table. It was a safe space. I loved going to "resource" even though some of the other children would jeer at me. The resource teacher was a tall man who once fell off his bicycle on his way to work and could not come for a few weeks. Those weeks were extra hard, as I had nothing to look forward to.

I believed others perceived me as fair game with no repercussions to their actions towards me. I remember on this particular day an older girl upped the ante, walked up to me, and stomped on my foot, then laughed and walked away. I burst into tears. The older boy, who, I felt, took pleasure in correcting my reading, had earlier appeared to think it would be funny to throw a basketball directly at my head during PE. I was feeling disoriented, but had become used to people pushing and shoving me. It was bad enough that I was not skilled at sports, and would trip and bang into things naturally. I was now regularly targeted.

I remember another day when this girl stood up on the desk and shouted, "I hate you, Hannah! You are nothing but a bitch! My mum hates you. Everyone does." At that, The Teacher came in, and the girl said, "It's true!"

The Teacher just said, "Get down," and she sat down and she was not reprimanded or asked to apologise.

I just sank into my desk, feeling really unsafe, starting to believe she might be right: I was broken. After all, nobody had corrected her or told me any different. All I wanted as a child was to fit in and have friends, but I did not feel safe in the school environment.

When I came home, I was very low, and Mum didn't take long in finding out what had happened. The next day, Mum tried to fix it, and came to school to express her concern and dissatisfaction as to how the situation was handled. She said that, as I was among the youngest in the class, the onus was on The Teacher to safeguard against this sort of behaviour. She asked The Teacher what they were going to do about it, but the response was that nothing needed to be done and that it would work its self out.

My maternal grandfather, who had Alzheimer's, was dying, and needed to have my mum looking after him a lot, so she was not around as often as she used to be. One day, I came into school and some of the children in the classroom had created an "I Hate Hannah Club". They would meet in an area in the schoolyard at the back of the shelters, and talk about all of the things that they hated about me, Hannah. I had one friend at the time who was never the most loyal. She said she was going to join the club so that she could find out what they were saying and tell me. I think by the end of it, she was the leader, as she had the most ammunition and could tell them the most things about me. Having spent lunch on my own, the following day I went to the group and was greeted with, "What are you doing here? This is an 'I Hate Hannah Club'," and I said, "Well, I hate Hannah too, so I should be able to join." They just laughed.

My dad was the one who had to deal with it when I came home. Dad has never been very good at dealing with stuff, so I am not quite sure how he handled it. Needless to say, the bullying situation did not improve. I became a bigger outsider, very low, and I couldn't take it anymore. This nastiness towards me went on for almost two years. It started small, and gradually peaked in the "I Hate Hannah Club". My parents tried again to get The Teacher to address these issues, but with no success. A few weeks later, Mum took me out of school and home-schooled me, due to the bullying and the unwillingness to support me and acknowledge my difficulties.

I've recently read a typed record with the dates and details of the meetings and correspondence that my parents had with The Teacher, the Board of Management, and finally the Department of Education. It was only in 2022 that I discovered this report existed. I sometimes feel angry that this bullying continued on a daily basis over a long period during a formative time in my life. All I know is it wasn't right and the impact of this trauma was to last.

*

One of the things that was suggested to my parents that would help me with my dyspraxia and my motor skills was ballet. I had started taking ballet classes when I went into third class. I'd always wanted to be a ballet dancer. I wasn't very good at dancing, and I had long, uncoordinated limbs, but I hoped I would grow into an elegant dancer, like the "ugly duckling" who grew into a "swan". One day at ballet, the teacher said, "Hannah, I said *point* your *left* toe." I knew she had said left, and I responded, "Yes, I know, I am telling my left toe to point, but it just won't." This was a regular occurrence when I was following directions or learning steps; I knew what I wanted and needed to do, but my ability to execute the command was unpredictable. The right toe sometimes would pop out, the left arm would go up, or nothing might happen, but I would be sitting there looking at my left toe, willing it to point. The more that I tried, the worse it was for me. I would literally be banging into people, or having pains in my joints trying to sit and do stretches and floor movements. I physically felt uncomfortable and dizzy as I tried to think, initiate, and complete what I was meant to do, and I could see it was just not happening for me the way it was for everyone else, which was so frustrating.

I came home from school one evening, threw myself on the bed, and declared, "I'm giving up ballet, Mum. I just can't be bad at another thing. It's too much." I had been trying to swim, ride a bike, and dance – all unsuccessfully. All things that were meant to sort out this dyspraxia, and all things I was bad at! This was also around the time of the Credit Union Quiz, the "I Hate Hannah Club", and my dyslexia diagnosis. The message that I was getting at that stage was that I was a failure. This was also when I, as a child, began needing everything to be very clean and particular. I had to have my bedspread smoothed and nobody was allowed to sit on my bed. I had set ideas about how things must be, which I suppose was my way of coping with the rest of my world being so undependable and uncontrollable. .

*

I was a real thinker. I would ruminate about stuff, and have difficulty falling asleep at night. To this day, I find that my brain is too switched on. As soon as I lie down and turn off the lights, and am being supported fully by the bed, I suddenly become awake and alert. My brain becomes very active and starts to process everything that has happened during the day; tons of visual images of my day flash before me and I start to analyse everything. It can easily take me a few hours before I finally go to sleep.

In my childhood, the time that I spent waiting to go to sleep was also mixed with anxieties, along with the scenes from my day. This was particularly stressful around the time of my diagnosis, ballet, and the "I Hate Hannah Club". At night, I would be unable to sleep because I would worry that nobody would be my friend tomorrow, that I would be pushed, that I would be asked to read, that I would break a pencil, that I would feel fidgety, and that I would get in trouble. I was constantly worried about everything. Some nights, it would build so much that I could no longer contain my feelings and I would burst into tears, and, sobbing, would make my way to Mum and Dad in the sitting room to seek their support. I think one of the things that really worked for me was that I was very much a talker. If I could talk out things, it diminished some of the fears for me, as I was no longer alone

39

with my worries. My mum and I made up the "What if" game to help me. We would think about different scenarios and make up a potential problem like, "What if I can't find my pencil?" Then we would work out my options; I could calmly empty out my bag and look for it; I could use my crayons; I could borrow a classmate's pencil; I could ask the resource teacher. This process enabled me to begin to address the worries. I stopped obsessing about them and it helped me to realise that everything was going to be okay. We also used the "What if" game to help me to plan for unforeseen situations. I needed to be taught some of the things that came naturally to others, to work through scenarios which didn't matter as much to others but were distressing to me. This was particularly relevant when I was faced with unplanned or unexpected things.

Mum did not like to see me so distressed, and tried to support me further to manage my "worries". She got me a bag of centimetre-sized matchstick people called "Worry People". She told me that I no longer had to worry on my own, and that I could whisper into the little dolls' ears and tell them all my worries, and that they would take the worries and worry for me. Every night, I would pick my six biggest worries and whisper them into each Worry Person, give them a little kiss, and place them under my pillow. I would have to space them out, otherwise the sensation of them under my pillow would hurt me when I slept. Sometimes, if I was feeling very dyspraxic and tactile, I would put them in a little bag beside my pillow so that the sensation of them under my pillow wouldn't disturb my sleep. At one stage, I got bigger Worry People: they were larger versions of my original tiny matchstick people with little turbans on their heads, each about two inches long. These were for my really big worries. Sometimes, if there was a massive worry, I would tell two or three of them about it so they could share the load, and this seemed to work a bit in helping me to fall asleep.

My mum used to have this pair of slippers when she was a little girl, and at the top was a circular little furry fluffy face with two wobbly eyes glued on. When my mum got too old for the slippers, she cut off the fuzzy faces to keep. I had a little sweet tin that I would keep one of the furry guys in, and whenever I felt really stressed, I would take it out of the tin and brush it forwards and backwards over my chin, and say, "It's going to be okay. It's going to be okay." That was one of my little calming techniques to help me cope.

*

I loved the idea of sleepovers. Movie references meant that I had a preconceived idea of what childhood was meant to be about – having friends and visiting their houses. There was only one problem: these events rarely met my expectations. I wasn't relaxed and happy; instead, I would often find it distressing. I would put a lot of pressure on myself to enjoy the sleepover, and then beat myself up for not being able to adapt and accept things as they were and just behave "normally". I would have unsuccessful sleepover trips, resulting in my being collected or dropped home in tears because I could not settle. I remember one time crying my eyes out and having to be dropped home after a failed sleepover at the house of my best friend at the time, Aisling. We were in school together, and we had been to each other's houses many times on playdates. Her mum had even braided yellow, orange, and pink strings with beads into a section

41

of my hair, just like Aisling's. We had planned our sleepover for ages, and all was going well; it was just like a normal playdate. We had our dinner, we made up dances, and I participated in Aisling's family's bedtime routines: supper, washing, teeth brushing, PJs, and book reading. Obviously, I am not a reader, so my bedtime routine was quite different. Aisling had the light on because she was reading, and I was trying to lie down and shut off, and it wasn't really working for me. I got upset, and could not at that stage understand or articulate properly what was actually upsetting me. Some of it was that I was not able to read like Aisling. This worry was added to all of my other worries, but I could not concentrate on them properly, as the light was on and I was getting overtired. As soon as the light went off, my brain went on high alert and it all became too much in unfamiliar surroundings. Worse, I didn't have my little Worry People. I began to sob. Aisling then became upset, and Aisling's mum came into the room to see what had happened. I was unable to calm down, so Aisling's mum reasoned that I must be homesick and should return home. I was not homesick; I was overwhelmed, and I could not process or articulate the problem.

Moments like this did not deter me from wanting to have and attend sleepovers. Some were more successful than others, and we managed to have some that didn't involve late-night/early-morning pickups.

I often need to do things at least twice before I have a successful outcome. It's like the first time I do something, it is the dress rehearsal. Then the second time is typically more successful, as I'm less anxious, can identify my triggers, and have thought of all of the "What if" game answers.

*

As Mum had taken me out of my second primary school, she was now having to home-school me while she secured a new school placement. I remember learning lots from my mum during those months of home-schooling. In the meantime, Mum took Anne's advice and applied for a place in Catherine McAuley's, the special reading school originally set up by a nun for kids like me with profound reading difficulties and dyslexia. I was offered a place following a couple of months of home-schooling, and started in the last month of that school year. There were eight classes, with each class comprised of up to 10 students. Most of the classes had a majority of boys (dyslexia tends to occur more frequently in males). In my new class, there were eight boys and one other girl called Sally.

Catherine McAuley's School was located in the centre of Dublin city. As we lived in the countryside towards the Meath border, the journey to Catherine McAuley's would take up to an hour and a half on public transport in the morning. Most students only attended the school for two years, and it focused solely on remedial work for children with dyslexia. This school did not follow the mainstream curriculum, as they did not teach Irish, and the week was broken up with lots of small group sessions and one-to-one time with support workers. The children who went to the school were from diverse backgrounds: in my class there was a little boy whose parents were in prison, and another little boy who was adopted from Africa; and in the class next door, there was a girl whose father was the CEO of a big company. This was so different to my past schools.

In order to attend Catherine McAuley's I had to get up very early in the mornings. My dad would sometimes drive me in, as at the time, he was working nearby. Other times, I would get the bus. But in the afternoons, I would always have to get two buses home. Ruth and Stuart were attending school in Meath, while Robert was still in the junior class of the local school. My little brother, Killian was in Montessori in Finglas, so it was impractical for Mum to pick me up from the city centre of Dublin. My route home consisted of the number 7 from outside of my school to the city centre, where I would then walk 20 minutes towards Busaras (central Dublin bus station) for my connecting bus. I was spending a large amount of time commuting and I was not street savvy.

Going to Catherine McAuley's and having that long commute meant that as a 10-year-old I was going around Dublin all on my own. One time, walking past the post office on O'Connell Street, people were protesting against abortion; as a 10-year-old, I was having pictures of foetuses shoved in my face and not quite understanding what it was all about. It especially didn't help that I was not able to read the signs.

There was one particular boy in my class who had a name for being a troublemaker. The Principal came into our class one day to reprimand him for misbehaving. I had never seen someone get shouted at the way she shouted at and disciplined him that day. I stood up in class and said, "Please leave him alone", and began to cry. I don't know why I tried to stand up for this boy, because he would never have done it for me, and in fact, he would often go out of his way to actively upset others. At any rate, I also found myself in the Principal's office that day for standing up for this boy, and she was not as friendly on this occasion as she had been on my first visit. I was in trouble for talking back to her, and she informed my parents that I was too sheltered and oversensitive.

Many kids from Catherine McAuley's would have to get to the city centre to catch their connecting bus home. You could take the number 7 bus from outside of Catherine McAuley's to the city centre of town. One day I got on the bus along with a group of classmates, including the troublemaker. The boy started misbehaving and the bus driver slammed on the brakes, opened the door, and kicked off all of the students from Catherine McAuley's, including me.

I said, "But I'm not with him."

The driver said, "You're all kicked off."

I again said, "I'm not doing anything wrong."

"Yes," he said, "but you're one of them."

We all walked towards the city centre of Dublin, not really sure where we were going. We walked in a pack, stopping every now and again to ask for directions. I was so late that I missed my connecting bus and Mum was furious with me that evening. This was before the days of mobile phones. I had tried to call on a payphone once I got to Busaras, but Mum had already left the house to collect me.

Generally, my commute was uneventful. Sometimes I had to take the number 11 bus to my mum in Ballymun. On one occasion, for some reason, the buses were not stopping where they usually did. Three buses had passed me but had not stopped. I noticed that there was a sign on the bus stop, but I was unable to decipher it. They had moved the bus stop. I didn't really know my way around town as a 10- or 11-year-old, and I was not sure what to do because I did not know where else I could get the bus from. I used a payphone to ring Mum's work; she was now working for a large organisation in Ballymun. The lady on the switch board said Mum wasn't there. I then explained the bus issue and my inability to read the sign. I guess the lady was concerned that a panicked 10-year-old was stuck in the city centre. She told me that I should wait where I was, and she would come and get me. I sat for an hour on the steps of Eason's bookshop on O'Connell Street until a lady I had never met approached me and asked, "Are you Hannah?" She read the sign, helped me find the alternative bus stop, and I managed to get on the bus to Ballymun to meet Mum.

Outside of school, I was attending weekly Speech and Drama classes with a lady named Ivy, who was a drama teacher in her fifties. There were four other girls, and we would sit on couches in her sitting room learning poetry and how to speak properly. Attending Catherine McAuley's School, I was mixing with a lot of children who were from the inner city who had strong Dublin accents, and I started to drop my "th"s. Ivy was adamant that I didn't do this; she was also adamant that her students were on time. We would do a lot of sight reading, which I never had to do; instead, I got to do an extra mime or learn an extra poem. I don't think I was her favourite because I never had my first choice of the characters in the monologues and poems; instead, I would usually get the part that I wasn't very excited by. Before I began attending Catherine McAuley's, my mum would drop me off at Ivy's for my class, but when I started at Catherine McAuley's, I would not be home in time for Mum to drop me, so I'd get the 123 bus to Ivy's from a different stop on O'Connell Street.

One Thursday when I was on the bus heading to Ivy's, there was an accident on the road ahead, and the bus was severely delayed because we were stuck in traffic. I started to panic, so I decided to go to the top of the bus to speak with the bus driver to fix this. Ivy would not tolerate tardiness, and if you were going to be late or not attend, she insisted that you call and notify her, or send your apologies. I convinced the driver to radio the bus depot with the number for Ivy, which I had written on a piece of paper, and tell Ivy that I was going to be late as I was stuck in traffic. Looking back on it now, it seems ridiculous, but I must have been very distressed to have convinced them to make this phone call. That day, Ivy picked up the phone to receive a call from a man informing her: "Hannah is stuck in traffic and won't be on time for her Speech and Drama class, and she sends her apologies." Not having mobile phones at the time meant that neither I nor the bus driver had the ability to call Ivy directly. Luckily, this was a once-off occurrence!

*

Mixing with different children at Catherine McAuley's was an eye opener, and I realised that I had been quite sheltered. We lived in the countryside and didn't really have neighbours, and I was suddenly mixing with people from inner-city flats who had free rein of their free time, and would often hang out and do what they wanted in the evening. One day, a girl started asking me about my "pussy". I was really confused, and said, "Oh, I don't have a pussy. Our neighbour has a pussy, and she has been a bit sick lately, but we don't have one." I was also introduced to

47

lots of new slang with double meanings, such as, "Will you meet him?" I would respond, "Okay. Meet him where?" which would be followed by laughter. Later, I realised that "meet" implies "French kiss." I guess I was vulnerable and naïve. I learned to be cautious and not to take situations at face value.

I made some good girl friends at Catherine McAuley's: my new friends were so different, but we all had dyslexia in common. One girl had the most amazing house, with a maid and gardener, and fancy food. It was just a world apart. Another friend lived in a council flat, and we ate microwave chips for dinner. The third girl's home life was similar to mine. The Spice Girls were popular at the time, and we used to get a cassette player and tape the Spice Girls song "If You Wanna Be My Lover" from the radio. We would play it and dress in bright-coloured clothes, belly tops, and crazy hair. I was always Baby Spice. One of the girls had curly hair, and she would be Scary Spice. Another of the girls, with quite sallow skin, would be Posh Spice, and the last girl got to be Ginger Spice. We would make up dance routines, and one afternoon we spent the whole afternoon practising our performance in the box room at my house. When we were happy with our routine, I had Mum get the video camera and film us doing our Spice Girl tribute. I had never had a group of friends before. It was so exciting. We shared everything and there was a collective energy and joy in having a supportive group of friends to which we belonged.

We all got on quite well, but the difficulty was with the school being based in town. One girl lived on the far, far south side of Dublin, over an hour away from my house. Another lived east, and a third lived out west near Celbridge, while I was very far on the north side. So we didn't socialise often, as it took lots of organising and lifts.

The school was beside the Bank of Ireland, and on one very windy day, the roof blew off the back of the bank. We were sent home early because it was very dangerous. Mum was due to pick me up that day, but, because the weather was so bad, she did not feel safe driving. She had tried to ring the school to let me know, but could not get through. One of my girlfriends was one of the few children who was collected from school, so Mum had contacted her father and asked him to let me know that I was to get the bus home. He told me this and then my eyes lit up as he gave me a pound to get a treat. When I got to Busaras, I spent my pound wisely on a can of Coke and a pack of Maltesers. I was so chuffed that I wished the roof would blow off the bank every day, so I could always have a pound and sit drinking my Coke and eating Maltesers in Busaras.

It was in Catherine McAuley's that I learned for the first time how to spell my name and address. I know it may sound crazy that, at the age of 11, I still could not do this. The teachers at the school did a lot of one-to-one work: I learnt the suffix "tion," and for the first time started to actually learn to spell some words. But I still wasn't reading. I learnt some key words in set situations, but could not decode them out of context. I'd hear words as images that I then translated to sounds: "tion" is the sound "shun". At Catherine McAuley's, I finally met other people just like me, people who had the same kind of difficulties I did. It was also a much more positive place as a learning environment, so I went from a schooling environment with little support to the opposite – an environment with supportive people who understood my difficulties. But even with this support, I was not doing well in terms of my reading and writing. The school psychologist said, "Don't force Hannah to spend all of her time on reading and writing. You can push Hannah to try to learn to read and write, and she may eventually become mediocre at reading and writing … Maybe. However, it is likely that this will become very frustrating and stressful. Instead of focusing all of your energy on trying to teach Hannah to read and write, you can invest all that time and resources into helping Hannah to be good at other things where she has huge potential." She suggested that we invest in drama, swimming, and other skills that were important to me.

Students typically stayed in Catherine McAuley's for two years, but after a year, we decided, with the support of the same school psychologist, that I would move, as it was unlikely that I would improve my reading and writing skills any further. I was exhausted from the long commute, and the main focus of my attending the school had been to support my literacy skills. Although reading is the main way that most people obtain information, and writing is often the chosen medium for communicating knowledge (especially in academic environments), I was beginning to realise that this would not be my route to accessing information and demonstrating knowledge, and I was comfortable with this. My year in Catherine McAuley's had taught me that there are many people who struggle with reading, for many reasons, just like me. When a student finished their time at Catherine McAuley's, they were given a little Oxford Dictionary as a parting gift. I still have mine, but I've never used it.

Robert was always better than me at everything. For example, he learned to ride a bike before me and was more skilful at it. We started to learn piano at the same time, and after only a couple of weeks, Robert was two grades ahead of me. I decided that it probably wasn't for me, and gave up the piano. Robert is a musical genius, and from a very early age he was adept at picking up instruments. He could play by ear, and went on to earn Master's degree in music. It is a huge part of him, but back then I guess I didn't see it that way; I just saw it as another thing that my little brother was superseding me at.

There was a badminton club in the community centre near us. We joined and got badminton rackets. Again, Robert, who is two and a half years younger than me (and three years younger academically), picked up badminton quite quickly, while I struggled.

My parents said that one night I stood there and spent the entire night bending down and picking up the shuttlecock, trying to serve. I just couldn't get the racket and the shuttlecock to make contact. Finally, after repeating this action multiple times, I was able to hit it over the net. My dad, who was watching me, said that he had never seen such determination in a child to stick at it and continue, regardless of the fact that it was soul-destroying that I wasn't able to even begin to play the game. I am sure that the person on the opposite side of the court found it frustrating and might not have wanted to be the person who had to play with that girl. With me.

It's difficult when someone younger surpasses you at everything that requires skill. I'd accepted that Stuart and Ruth would be more skilled than me because they were older. I found it harder to cope with being surpassed by a younger sibling. Again, I had set ideas of how life worked. I think that's quite common; a lot of the children and teenagers whom I have worked with, who have siblings who don't have dyspraxia, often struggle with the fact that their younger siblings are more talented and skilled in multiple areas. I loved that my brother Killian was different like me. I always had a special affinity with him: although we had our different challenges, we both had to carve out our own way.

*

I was never very good at gauging distance. My spatial awareness was appalling. My mum didn't have the best spatial awareness either. Mum was a bit of a nervous driver, especially when it came to parking. She would often ask us to look out the back window and tell her how far back she could go. I could not even begin to imagine how far back she could go.

When I was very little, Mum would say, "Well, would a skinny person fit? Or a fat person? Or a medium person?" And that was how we gauged it.

I would say, "Yeah, Mum! Go back! One fat person and a skinny person!"

On one occasion, we were on holiday in France and were parking the car. Mum was asking me how far back we could go.

I started shouting, "Two fat people! One fat person and a skinny-ish person!"

At that, there was an American couple, who were large and wearing fanny packs and sun caps, standing by the side of the road. The man looked disgusted as he approached the car. At that stage, Ruth said, "Hannah, they think you are talking about them."

I lowered my voice, and we wound up the window and scurried out.

From then on, Mum and I decided that it was probably a better idea, rather than saying "two fat people and one skinny person", to just say "two Hannahs" (instead of skinny people) and "two Mums", etc.

We all started swimming lessons in St Vincent's pool as babies from two years and up. Mum would always bring us to the seaside and encourage us to get in and jump over the waves, again from the age of two up. My mum took us to swimming lessons as soon as they would let you start. As a result, my siblings were all very good swimmers. I was not, but I was a determined child. My old swimming coach used to say that I was a horse of a girl and that he wasn't sure what I was doing in the water, but it certainly wasn't swimming. I would keep trying week after week, attempting to keep up with the others even if not gracefully. I used to start swimming in one lane and would end up in another lane. I would often get concussion from mis-gauging the distance between the swimming pool edge and where I was, ploughing myself into the side of the pool.

One day, a swim teacher took me aside and said, "You have to think about swimming in terms of pulling a rope" – as in one hand goes first and then the next. What he was saying just clicked for me, and suddenly, I was swimming a lot straighter and was able to stay in my own lane. I could move my body parts in sequence; I could breathe and I was coordinated. Now there was no stopping me!

*

Robert was moving up to the class where The Teacher was still teaching. Mum was keen to move him, so she was looking for a school that we could both attend along with my baby brother, Killian. We all got a place in the other local national school that was up the road in a different direction from our house. At that stage, Killian was also starting in the infants class there, so Mum wanted me to be there to help support him.

At lunch breaks, I would go in and help Killian if he needed his pull-up changed, or would communicate for him, and that was really lovely because it gave me a safe "out space" and facilitated Killian to go to a mainstream school for that year. Robert was there, too, so finally it was a bit easier for Mum, having her children in two separate schools rather than four. I was in sixth class and I had the Headmaster teaching me. He was a total contrast to The Teacher; he was fair, had firm boundaries, and was consistent. I was a novelty, I suppose, to my classmates, as I was suddenly coming into the class in which they had been together since they were four, and now as 11-year-olds there was a new girl. They also had a big focus on Gaelic Games and they needed girls to play on the football team, and you were allowed to use your hands. I was getting a bit more confident in terms of trying new things, because my experience in swimming and other activities had been a bit more positive. Now, I had a bit more self-belief and was willing to try stuff again.

Although I had an Irish exemption due to my dyslexia, I decided I wanted to participate in the Irish in class. I didn't have to do the reading and writing aspects, but I loved speaking the language. I had a good grasp of spoken Irish having gone to the Irish-speaking playschool and the Gaelscoil for the first three years. On one occasion, I won £1 in class, as I was able to say 20 sentences without using the same verb twice. I took pride in the fact that I was able to speak my national language. This experience was such a contrast to my time with The Teacher where I never won anything nor was I praised.

When I was in sixth class, I went on an aeroplane for the first time. Our neighbour had kids my age, and the family had relocated to Germany where their dad had got a job. For my birthday, Mum booked me a flight to Germany to visit them. Back then, the airports were very different: all visitors went through security at the front doors. This meant that Mum was able to see me onto the plane. I bought a little teddy bear in Duty Free with my holiday money. I don't think the airline that I went with had a service to chaperone minors; instead, we were chatting with a lady while we were queuing for the aeroplane, and Mum asked, "Will you keep an eye on Hannah?" to which the lady agreed. I sat with my teddy on the plane beside this lady and she shared her Toblerone chocolate with me. At the other end of the journey, our former neighbour met me and we collected my bag together. This might not have been a major event for others, but for me it was my first ever flight and I got to go to Germany.

Finally, things were looking up. Life was becoming quite exciting. Having had lots of life experience at Catherine McAuley's, and as result of the various situations I found myself in, I had become more resilient. In addition, the upheaval of changing schools four times and having to start from scratch each time with some new baggage meant I had to develop skills and confidence in myself to deal with the next big adventure life would have for me.

Chapter Two: Teenage Years

Never renege on your potential and settle for mediocre as a call from the refuge.

- *Anam Cara, John O' Donoghue*

This is the *coming of age* chapter of my life. I started to walk into some familiar mistakes, but I had found my voice and I was approaching life with more optimism. In some ways, these years were the most challenging, and I was still being scaffolded by the support of my mother, teachers, and others.

As a teenager, I couldn't wait to develop a chest and have a bra. Some girls in my class were curvier and developed earlier. I got Mum to agree to buy me a bra, which was a 28AA training bra, in Roches Stores, which used to be on Henry Street. This expensive undergarment spent more time in my top drawer than on me. In spite of my initial excitement and desire for a bra, I soon realised that this was a mistake. I found it particularly difficult to wear bras. I couldn't stand the underwire and the tightness of a bra. To this day, I can become fixated on the sensation and feel it rubbing under my armpits and restricting me. I am also quite slight, and bony, so the wire can push in on my chest, leaving a sore mark.

I also couldn't tolerate having my teeth brushed. There were multiple rows with Mum about it, but I would still avoid doing it. I would even do things like wet the toothbrush and put it back just so I didn't have to brush my teeth. One day when I was 13, we were having a sleepover. I no longer needed my mum to come and pick me up. I could manage myself better, and girls loved to talk all night, which suited me, as I was good at this, too! Two girls from my secondary school were staying over at mine. They had both brushed their teeth and gone to bed. We were all sharing a double futon that was in the sitting room where we could watch a movie on the TV. One of the girls said I needed to re-brush my teeth, as I had bad breath. I quickly replied, "Oh, I hate brushing my teeth. I don't brush my teeth."

The girls turned around and said, "Hannah, that is so disgusting!" and looked appalled. Needless to say, at that point I felt really upset about the fact that my friends would have that opinion of me. I got up, found a toothbrush, and brushed my teeth, before returning to the futon to re-join the sleepover.

It wasn't that bad. I liked how my teeth felt after I had brushed them, and I liked being accepted.

So from then on, I thought it was time that I should start brushing my teeth, and would somehow have to start tolerating this sensation. Up to that point, the need to brush my teeth wasn't that great, but the discomfort of brushing my teeth was; I wasn't really motivated to brush my teeth because of the sensation of hard bristles against my mouth. Even trying to hold the toothbrush was challenging: I used to get achy pains when I would hold the toothbrush still, and when I'd twirl it. It would always end up staying in the one place, and my gums would feel quite sore, too. But after that night, I started to brush my teeth twice daily, and I would spend probably about four minutes at a time brushing my teeth quite thoroughly. It was very important that I had clean teeth so that I would be invited to the next sleepover.

*

We often went camping in France for our summer holidays. All of us piled into a family estate car with two tents (sometimes just one), and would drive down to Rosslare in Wexford and take the ferry overnight to Cherbourg. Once or twice, when we were very lucky, we would get a four-bed cabin on the ferry that we would all pile into. On one occasion that we had the cabin, I had just seen *Titanic*, and I was convinced that the ferry was sinking, as when you flushed the toilet, it went "sssssshhhhh!" sounding like a flood was coming in; so I actually slept better when we weren't in a cabin.

We would get to France, tired, after having travelled on the boat, and would pitch our tent and stay at a campsite. The campsites were quite fancy in France: they had shower facilities, and often had swimming pools and barbecue areas.

When we got a bit older, we would stay at Key camp holiday resorts, where there were tents with beds already there.

Every holiday, there would be a different person or group of people we would make friends with. They would usually be girls when I was younger, and then when I was probably about 14, we would make friends with boys and girls. There was always someone you had a holiday crush on.

One holiday, Ruth and I made friends with two Irish teenagers, who were the only English-speaking teens at the campsite. One night when we were hanging out at the bar by the pool, I announced to everybody, "I don't shave my legs. I don't have hair on my legs, because I have blonde hair."

Clearly I had very blonde hair on my legs, so I had hair on my legs, but my mum had told me from a young age that you shouldn't shave your legs because the hair will grow back black and bushy. She said it was better not to shave, and she regretted that she'd shaved when she was young. I think this was just something that she told me so I wouldn't try to shave at the age of 12 and get lots of cuts on my knees, being as clumsy as I am.

The guys just turned around and said, "Ugh!", as did Ruth, who went bright red and was embarrassed to be in my company. Needless to say, a couple of months later I did start shaving.

*

For secondary school, I went to a local mixed community school where Ruth and Stuart were also students. This was a much larger school with multiple classes in each year. I was confident in making friends but still had some gaps when it came to social skills. I made friends with a group of girls who were in my class, and at first we all got on really well. But something changed towards Christmas time; it started with them criticising the way that I sang, saying that I sounded like a sheep. This actually was based on a comment made by a teacher who said that I put too much vibrato in my voice, and then did an impression of me that sounded like a sheep. From then on this became a running "joke", but one that I found quite hurtful. They also stopped inviting me out with them, and said it was because I didn't drink or smoke, which was a bit silly because they didn't really drink or smoke either.

In Religion class, there were rows of two and three tables; I would always sit beside two of the girls.

One day, one of these girls said, "Oh, that chair is being kept for a different girl" – a girl who wasn't at school that day.

I said, "Well, she isn't in today"

She said, "She might be in later so I'm keeping it for her."

The girls, for some reason, started to do more of these exclusionary things and say little hurtful comments. I tried to address it head on and pull them up on it, like saying, "That girl is not in today", or "Please stop saying that. I don't find it funny". They would always be giggling when I would come over and then stop talking, and not really make space for me by the radiator at lunch. It got to a stage where I was feeling very down and Mum was concerned. Mum actually wrote a letter to the Year Head to say what had been going on, that the group were going out of their way to say mean things and exclude me, and the effect this was having on me. After that, some of the girls apologised and everything was fine. The rest stopped the nasty behaviour, but needless to say, they weren't friends any more.

I started hanging around with a girl who was a year below me in secondary school. She had been making glasses for an entrepreneur project, and she made me one with "Hannah" on it, which was quite nice. We would socialise sometimes at lunch by the radiator, and also outside of school. She moved to Wexford in third year but still remained a good friend of mine. At the same time she left, a new girl moved to our school in third year. We hung out a lot as well. She was a quiet girl, and we didn't really socialise at each other's houses that much, but she did invite me to a couple of events, and she did come to my house once or twice.

*

One of the things that we did when I first started secondary school was to talk to the Resource Teacher. We explained that when I received homework, it shouldn't be marked with red pens.

I had a visceral reaction to red lines, probably because, in my days in the local primary school, most of my work would have nothing but red lines all the way through it. This made me feel very stressed, like I had failed in every way, and I would hone in on the fact that I couldn't spell and my handwriting was not great. Even if I typed the work, there would be lines on every word or every other word.

Part of secondary school involved having multiple teachers for multiple subjects. Although the Resource Teacher had a copy of my report, I would often have to go up and explain my needs to the individual teachers. I would mainly clarify that I didn't take notes but that I would still be concentrating. I would also ask if I could have a copy of the acetates which they put up on the projector. Everyone would sit in class and copy the notes from the acetates into their books to learn from, and I needed teachers to photocopy these for me. If I got the copies before the class, it was best, because I could then highlight my copy and draw little symbols on parts that I really needed to learn or remember, but it also meant that I could store the information that was being read in class and commit it to memory.

Sometimes, teachers would forget or there would be a substitute teacher in, and they would say things like, "Hannah, read the next paragraph."

I would have to say, "Can Tom read it instead?" – or whoever was sitting beside me – in order to remind them that this was not going to be possible.

Similarly, if we were told in class to read a comprehension assignment and answer the questions, more of a reading task instead of a lecture or interactive exercise, I would turn to the person beside me and see if we could do it (at least the reading component) together.

In one English class, I didn't have my copybook. I had scribbled down my homework assignment and handed it in on a sheet.

The teacher said to the class, "Who owns this?" When I put my hand up, she scribbled on it with a pencil, gave it a C, and handed it back to me. I noticed that the sheet had something written on it in pen on the bottom, which then had lines scratched out on top of it in pencil. I got an eraser and rubbed out the pencil to see what was written underneath, then asked a classmate to read it to me.

It said, *"Will not read this work until you do it again neater."*

This upset me. I wondered if that particular teacher had never read my work, had just decided that I must be a C or D student, and had graded me accordingly. I often got better grades after I got a computer and I began typing out some of my assignments. In fact, I was sent on a typing course when I was in third or fourth year. During Irish lessons, which I didn't do because of my exemption, I would learn how to type with a typing teacher. It was ASDF JK; with the two middle ones being F and J. You used the tactile cue of the raised bit on F and J to navigate the keys. I found this really boring, because I would have to repeat sentences and copy from a sheet, typing them on the computer over and over. There was a method to the monotonous activity, however, as eventually I discovered I could now touch type. This helped with some of the legibility issues with my handwriting, but unfortunately I still didn't know how to begin to begin to start or to spell half of the words that I wanted to. I often found that I would choose to type a shorter, simpler word, as I didn't know how to spell the longer, more complicated word. For example, I might have said "sad" instead of "disappointed", as I was unable to imagine how to spell the latter. Unfortunately, I was often forced to use words with a slightly different and less detailed meaning. But sometimes I just had to settle for less.

*

I was sitting in Irish class one afternoon, which was a double class, beside a guy. He was one of those teenage boys who had acne and unkempt hair. The teacher was stern and direct. In the middle of the class, this big whistling fart was heard, and the teacher turned around and said, "Who owns that!"

I shoved my hand up and said, "I did it!"

Everybody just looked at me, probably thinking, *What on earth? Why would you admit to it?* It wasn't smelly or anything; it was just so strangely loud, and it had made a whistling sound.

Afterwards, everyone said, "Hannah, you had the perfect alibi – you could have said nothing! You were sitting beside one of the smelliest guys in the class!"

I couldn't blame him as it was wrong and it wouldn't be fair on him. I always had a very strong sense of justice and took ownership of my actions, whether they were right or wrong. Luckily, it didn't end up in the yearbook; they had other stories to put in.

*

The school was putting on a performance of *Fiddler on the Roof* one Christmas. I decided I wanted to audition for it and I had initially been cast in a small part playing the dead wife who comes back and screams at her husband in a dream. An older girl was cast as Hodel, one of the daughters. For some reason, that girl pulled out of the Hodel role, and I ended up getting this lead role in the musical. I was so proud and excited, because I loved acting and now I could actually perform at school.

I was playing opposite a boy called Tom, who was my stage husband, and I had to do a dance routine with him; it was a simple routine, but I found it difficult to coordinate moves, especially with other people. Added to this, I didn't know Tom that well. I was getting very stressed about this dance, afraid I was going to mess up on stage. So my mum suggested I invite Tom over to my house and practise. I asked Tom in school the next day, and to my surprise he agreed. He was also worried the dance routine wasn't going so well. Two days later, Tom got the bus with me to my house and we hung out, but mainly we just practised and practised our dance, which consisted of bumping heads, nervous laughter, and standing on feet. It was less stressful practising without people watching, and best of all, we got to eat pizza.

On the night of the musical, we did a great job. Although we were a bit rigid, our steps were correct, and it was so much fun getting to be good at something connected to school. It helped strengthen my friendship with Tom, and he turned out to be very supportive. After that point, he would read for me in English class, too. I'm so lucky that the world is full of kind people.

*

I loved going to lifesaving lessons. I would imagine that I was going to be a lifeguard in *Baywatch* someday. Stuart was the first to start and when I became old enough to go, I jumped at the chance. It wasn't just swimming; I also learned how to throw ropes (where you would coil up a rope and throw it out to pull someone in), first aid, and water incidents (which is like doing first aid or emergency care in the water, but everyone was only acting and we were always timed).

The first few competitions I entered, my partner and I placed second to last. We came fourth in the third competition that we entered. I continued to persist, train, and try harder, and in 2000, my new partner Niamh and I came first in the Republic of Ireland and we got to go to the Northern Ireland Championships. We went to Belfast and entered the competition again. We were shocked, because we actually won! Each year, the people who won in Belfast went on to represent Ireland in the National Life Saving Competitions in the UK. We ended up placing fourth in the National competition.

The following year, we re-entered and got through to the UK competition again. When we'd finished, Niamh and I thought we'd done really well, perhaps even placing third. The names for third and second place were announced, but ours weren't called. We'd given up hope by that point. And then first place was announced: "Hannah and Niamh". I could not believe it! I started bawling, doubling up with emotion, trying to stand on the platform and accept my trophy.

I guess I had learned to lose gracefully, but hadn't quite mastered how to win, and was unable to process my emotions. It made me realise that the girl who flounders and knocks into others in the swimming pool can become a champion lifesaver. There were moments when I had been injured in lifesaving classes, or seeing my younger brother surpass me in lots of ways, and I would think, *Why am I bothering doing this every Sunday night and Thursday evening?* But in the end, it was worth it. Our names were engraved on a huge plaque and we received gold medals. I was proud as punch, and couldn't sleep because I had so much adrenaline going through me. The head of the swimming club (who had called me a "horse of a girl") wrote me a lovely letter telling me how proud he was, and that Niamh and I had brought so much joy to our club. He remarked that I had learnt to swim in the club and was now an athlete. He noted it was the first time that Ireland had ever won the Junior Girls Lifesaving Competition; our names were the first Irish names engraved on this large trophy.

*

In the first year of secondary school, when I was 13, there were discos in the local GAA Club, called the "Wotton". You would pay a few pounds to go to this disco, and you could buy a can of Coke or 7up inside. And, they played real dance music.

Only a few of my friends were allowed to go to these discos. I was obsessed with the TV show *Ally McBeal* at that age. The show was about a lawyer called Ally who always wore suits with exceptionally short skirts. I somehow convinced Mum to buy me a little short suit skirt, and I would wear it with belly tops to go to these discos.

You would go and kiss lots of different boys that you knew. It was quite innocent, really. The venue was spacious, but everyone tended to huddle together and it was dark. As you know, I am not the most coordinated person at the best of times, and one night I accidentally knocked into a girl called Jane, spilling my full can of fizzy drink on her. Jane was quite intimidating; she was tall and broad. Anyway, I said sorry and ran off.

But then on Monday in school, there was a rumour circulating that Jane was going to hop on me. First I had to find out what the word "hop" meant: I quickly became educated and realised "hop" meant "fight", and that Jane was going to beat me up. I was a twig-like teenager, quite naïve, who would cry when people shouted, and now I was going to be "hopped" on. I was friends with another girl who had a sister a couple of years older than us. Her sister circulated another rumour that if Jane hopped on me, then she would hop on Jane. Nothing actually happened in the end, but at the time, I had a few days when I was worried and didn't want to get into trouble, all over a silly can of fizzy drink. I don't know whether Jane just disliked me (I was a bit of an annoying goody-two-shoes), or if it was just because I happened to be very clumsy and spilled some fizzy drink on her at a disco.

I was also not sure how everyone else seemed so much more clued in to these social rules and ways. I felt like I needed to learn them all the hard way. I think people read about stuff or were more observant about how things are. There was a radio show called *Adrian Kennedy Phone Show*, which had discussions of all kinds of controversial issues. A few of the girls would listen to the show on their radio alarm clocks in their bedrooms. There was one episode about virgins and whether people should wait to have sex until after marriage. Even though I knew from a very young age how babies were made (as a result of taking Jessie to the stud), I went home after we had discussed this in school and asked Mum, "Mum, are you a virgin?"

"Don't be ridiculous, Hannah!" she said. "How is that possible?"

I was kind of confused for a while. I said, "But, did you have sex before marriage?"

Mum didn't answer that question, but she did say, "Hannah, a virgin is someone who has never had sex. So if I had never had sex, then I would never have had you, would I?"

I was happy kissing a boy or two that I liked at the Wotton, but that was all. One night at the disco, I was kissing a boy I knew from school. He was a year ahead of me, but I knew him to see and say hi to. While we were kissing, this guy stuck his hands up my top. I felt so uncomfortable and got really upset. I said, "You have no right to touch me!" I was very upset by the incident, which was probably quite innocent, but I took it personally. It was not something I had consented to, and it was new and unpredictable.

Later, I realised this was more of a sensory aversion for me as opposed to anything else.

*

I was 14 and the meningitis vaccination had come out. We all needed signed permission slips to receive the vaccination, which we were given in school. Before the vaccination, my mum was anxious because she had heard about people having reactions to the injection, so she was of two minds as to whether or not I should receive it. But Mum signed my permission slip and told me to ask questions about the vaccine; if I then felt I wanted to get it, I could produce my permission slip.

I asked the nurses a few things about the vaccine while we were waiting, and felt quite confident that actually it was okay, as most of my classmates were also getting it. The administration of the injection was done so that all of the girls from a given year were brought in and vaccinated, and then sent back to class. The next group was going to be the boys. Because I had been a bit anxious about receiving it, the nurse suggested I wait until the end, so everybody would get their vaccination and I would get it last.

I went up to get my vaccination at the end, and as soon as the needle went in, I fell off of the chair. A little later, I woke up with my legs raised on a square plastic box in the library, surrounded by all of the boys. I was mortified because I was convinced that everyone could see my underwear; also, I was disorientated.

The reason that I fainted, which was explained to me, did not have anything to do with the actual injection, but was because I was so anxious and tense that I was holding my breath while receiving the injection and had worked myself up.

After that, I developed a slight fear of injections and needles. I put off getting my hepatitis shots for as long as possible because I just hated it, and even then I would always bring a friend or parent with me to get the injection because I was afraid I would faint and have to lie down, do deep breathing, and look the other way.

Shortly after my fainting incident, there was a modelling competition for a magazine called *Sugar*. The magazine had a search in the UK and Ireland, looking for the next modelling face. They were going to a shopping centre in Dublin, and Mum agreed to take us to the event. There was a stage and an area where they were doing some promotional stuff. One of the promotions they ran was where they would pick people from the audience, or you could volunteer to come and enter competitions and win prizes. I got up and volunteered myself for a dancing competition; you did a dance-off to some music, and they would pick a winner. There was a lot of Maybelline makeup on offer for the winner. I just got up and did the craziest moves I could think of, trying everything, including breakdancing, with such conviction that they decided that I had won. I was really excited to receive a big bag of Maybelline makeup as my prize. The other girls from my school were at the event, but I didn't know them, as they were in different classes and years to me.

The next Monday in school, loads of people came up to me and said, "You're the girl who danced!" Looking back on it now, they might have actually been mocking me, or maybe they thought I was just mad as a brush. But I had no sense of inhibition, and was very happy to get up there and do my best; I so wanted to just engage and be part of stuff, plus I now had my own makeup!

*

My Junior Cert state exams were my first time actually really doing any exams. I had not done first- or second-year exams in school, as I was not able to access them on my own, and the school did not give me readers or scribes. For my mock exam (pre-exam), I had some readers and scribes, who were teachers or Special Needs Assistants, I often mispronounce words (also known as verbal dyspraxia). This particularly happens to me when I am very tired, or if I can't fully visualise a word or remember how it sounds. For example, in my Junior Cert paper for Home Economics, one of the questions was, "How has the education system changed in Ireland from the 1980s to today?" My answer was, "In Ireland they got rid of the inter*course* and replaced it with the Junior Cert." What I had actually meant to say was that they had got rid of the Inter *Cert* (the old equivalent of the Junior Cert). My scribe looked up at me, and with no context for what I was trying to say, said, "Can I repeat that to you?"

I said, "No, no. I am under too much pressure for time. Let's move on."

It was only after I had completed the exam paper I asked the Scribe to read back over my answers. As she read, I heard her say, "They got rid of intercourse". At hearing that I said, "You can't say that!"

She replied, "Well, that's what *you* said!"

"No, I mean Inter Cert". We both started laughing and I asked her to change it.

Although I had never formally used readers and scribes up to my Junior Cert, my mum would often be my scribe and reader when it came to homework. Obviously, a homework assignment is 20 minutes or half an hour, and is a very different process to an examination. I wasn't used to dictating continuously for that long.

I also need to move around when I dictate. It helps me form ideas and create a rhythm. The words tend to flow better, and I can process things when I move. At home, I would always sit on the kitchen table, dangling my legs, moving around, and fidgeting; it would help me to listen and concentrate. In my Junior Cert, I found that I needed to do the same, so in my mock exam, some of the scribes would say, "Oh, you have to sit still. You cannot be moving about." I actually found that I needed to move about, because when I sat still, I couldn't take in the information and would become fatigued trying not to move. I find it difficult to maintain a fixed posture. I experience joint pains in my shoulders in particular. I get increasingly frustrated, and am so focused on trying to control my body and maintain a posture that I cannot possibly think about listening to information and processing it. I also cannot give accurate and structured responses or directions verbally when I'm not moving.

In the actual Junior Cert exam, I had scribes and readers, but they were provided by the State, and my exams were tape-recorded. I was, however, allowed to move around the room. I actually got four As, four Bs, one C, all on honours papers, and I think it was the first time that my teachers had an accurate understanding of where my ability and level actually was. Up to that point, they were never sure where I stood academically, because I didn't do exams, and often I wouldn't have done the homework, either. Occasionally, I would try to scribble something down on a sheet for an assignment, but it wasn't necessarily about it being coherent or legible, more to show that I was trying and because I had to hand in something – anything. Other times, Mum would type or handwrite a particularly important assignment. The Junior Cert was the first time that I actually got my real grades and I felt very proud of myself, which wasn't something that I often felt in terms of academic achievement.

For my Junior Cert, I was studying *Romeo and Juliet*. Mum had found a copy of it in the library on cassette, and I was so excited that I was going to be able to access my coursework on my own. Mum had bought me a Walkman, so I put the tape in and sat on the bus listening to about an hour of the play. I came home and listened to the other hour, and the next day listened to the next cassette, finishing the entire play in less than two days. I was chuffed with myself.

I said to Mum, "I've just read a whole play!"

"That's wonderful!" said Mum. "What was it about?"

It was then that I realised that I didn't actually take in any of the information I had heard because I hadn't trained myself to perceive information purely by audio. Until then, even though Mum would have read stuff to me, I would have sat with her and we would have discussed it, and I would have seen pictures; it was a very whole-sensory learning experience. So this new challenge for me was that, yes, it was accessible in some ways, but I had to train myself to process information purely through an aural method.

Having attempted to listen to the first tape multiple times, and only being able to partly retain the information, I then asked myself, *How do I learn?* It is multifaceted and multisensory for me, but I am also very visual. I realised at this stage that I associate words with imagery. By translating every word that I was hearing into a visual picture, I was able to understand it, but also retain the information in a rich way. Additionally, I tend to tag images to emotions. For example, in *Romeo and Juliet*, there is a scene where a character says, "Do you bite your thumb at us, sir?" This would have been the equivalent of how frustrating it would feel if someone stuck their fingers up at you. The characters were then provoked into fighting. By understanding what is meant, and by visualising it and tagging the emotion to it, I was able to feel and understand. The text came alive to me, so much so that now over 20 years later, I can still remember the line, "Do you bite your thumb at us, sir?"

I learned a lot about my learning style at that stage. In Art class, we learned about the Mona Lisa, and how it was famous because of her enigmatic smile. Even now, when I hear the word "enigmatic", I visualise the Mona Lisa's smile. "Symbiotic" is another word that my friend Tom and I used to talk about. He would always help me with my reading. When I hear "symbiotic", I think of an elephant with a bird on it, and the bird picking food off the elephant; the bird has food to eat, and the elephant is cleaned. There are a lot of other words like that. Almost every word that I say has some association to an image.

*

When I was 16, I decided I would take French as one of the subjects for my Leaving Cert. Mum knew a lady whose cousin lived in Caen, France at the time. He was married and had three kids, and his wife was expecting another baby. We arranged that I would go to France and work as an au pair for them for two weeks over the Easter break, and again during the summer.

Lots of preparation went into this trip: I learned some key sentences like "*Ou prendre le train a Caen?*", and how to get from the airport to Caen and generally find my way around. I had started seeing a boy in the year above me, and was a bit disappointed that I would be away for all of the Easter holidays.

I went to France and found my way to the train station, but decided not to take public transport in case I got it completely wrong. I had booked a ticket on a set train, so I was going to come into the train station at Caen and have the French family meet me. I didn't have a mobile phone at the time, though I did have the family's home number written in my little notebook.

I got to Paris and found the Gare du Nord station, and got on my train. I was starting to feel anxious about where I was going to go, and maybe my French wouldn't be good enough. I thought maybe the family wouldn't like me, as we had only exchanged one or two emails up to that point.

I finally arrived at the local station and was met by them all – the mum, a two-month-old baby, a two-year-old, a seven-year-old, and an eight-year-old. They drove me to their period townhouse. I was staying in the room that belonged to the girl who was eight, while she would share with her brother. That first night, though, I was trying to process everything from my day and felt overwhelmed. I remember crying at the mum that I was there to help her make her life easier and there I was so upset. But luckily for them, once I had my cry and processed my journey, I settled into my role quickly, as I was very experienced and a natural at playing with and minding kids.

For most of the two weeks I was in France, the two-year-old boy had *varicella* – "chicken pox". Although it was a really good life experience, I decided that I definitely wasn't going to have babies any time soon. I also was disappointed when I realised that my French was not as fluent as I thought it was. I'd thought I was fluent because I could understand what the eight-year-old girl would say to me. But one evening, her mother said, "Stop speaking in words, and speak in sentences!"

I did come back to Ireland with some interesting phrases because of the chicken pox, like *"Tu ne pas grater ta zizi,"* meaning, "You must not scratch your little boy bits." Needless to say, phrases like this would not be useful in my Leaving Cert exams, which had been the main reason for au pairing.

I came back after my two weeks exhausted, and I had missed out on spending time with my boyfriend, so I decided that I didn't want to return as the family's au pair the following summer. I sent an email saying I wouldn't be returning in the summer. And then, about two weeks later, I broke up with my boyfriend. Now, as an adult, I regret that I didn't go back and immerse myself in the language more.

*

When I had just turned 17, we were studying *Macbeth* in English class for our Leaving Cert. We were given a class assignment to compare the characters in *Macbeth* to characters in another text we had read in our spare time. When I got home after school, I was very grumpy, and flung my bag on my bed. Mum asked me when I was going to do my homework, and I said, "I'm not going to do it. I can't do it, as I haven't ever read a novel!" I had only listened to *Romeo and Juliet* and other set texts on the school curriculum.

Mum said, "Well, instead of a novel, why don't you use any book that you have read?"

I had only ever read short, simple books, but did my homework using one of them.

The next day, I handed in my assignment. At the end of the class, my teacher said, "I have one essay I have to read out. I could not believe the essay when I read it and I need to share it with the class. It was something that stood out."

I automatically cringed and shrank into my seat, thinking that she was going to ridicule me about only having been able to read simple books, but she said it was genius, and had given me an A. I had compared the relationship between Duncan and Macbeth to the relationship between the Sly Fox and the Gingerbread Man, bringing in the ideas of deceit and being lured into a sense of security. I remember thinking at that moment, *It doesn't really matter that I haven't done things the exact same way as everyone else. I am resourceful, and I can use what I do have. It is enough. It is just about figuring out how to use what I have.*

*

Around that time, I attended evening classes in Art History, English Studies, and Drama in town at Trinity College. I would go in the evenings, and sit in lecture halls with adults listening to university professors giving talks about subjects like Renaissance art. As a result, my week was pretty jammed; I would finish school, jump on a bus into the city centre, go to the library in town and access a book on tape, go to the evening lecture and then head off and get the bus home at nine o'clock most evenings. In school at that time, most of my peers would stay after school for two to three hours in what was called "supervised study", where their parents would pay for them to be supervised by teachers so that they would do their homework and study for their exams. This was something that was never accessible to me, due to the nature of sitting at a desk and also having no one to read the material to me. The reason I went to Trinity at night time with adults was because it was one way of my accessing information in a way I could grasp, and it helped to reinforce my studies. I was doing English at the time, as well as Art, which has a History element to it, too.

*

There is a private boy's secondary school on the northside of Dublin that had a reputation for putting on really good musicals and Shakespearean plays. The school had its own theatre with a proper stage. Some of the students would take on the role of building sets, and they would hire costumes. There was a musical director, who has since passed away, who was famous for doing these musicals and plays.

Because it was an all-male school, they often got girls in to play the female roles in their productions. The majority of the girls usually came from an equivalent female private school in the city centre. Our neighbour up the road was friends with the musical director and asked him if it would be okay if I auditioned for the productions as well, and he was happy for me to do so. There were a couple of other people who were sisters of the boys who attended the school, or friends of friends, who were also offered auditions for the productions.

The year I was old enough to audition, the production was *Crazy for You*, a musical by the Gershwin brothers. By the time I was asked, all of the lead roles had been given away (not that I would have necessarily gotten one), but there were positions in the chorus, so I got a part there.

The cast had to learn dance routines and singing parts, and it was great fun. We did five nights of the show. I had a bright blue satin silk skirt and a big hat. They wanted our hair curled, and because mine is poker straight and so fine, it took a lot of effort to curl; Mum put starch in my hair and tightly rolled it each night, which meant I found it hard to sleep because of the sensation, but I loved to perform, so I felt it was worth it in the end.

The following year, they were putting on a production of *Tom Jones*, and I auditioned for a part in it. I hadn't actually read the whole script, and for the part I auditioned for, I had to start shouting, "You fiend! You trollop! I'll kill you!" For this character, I had to act out a scene where I collapsed, which I thought was because the character had just fainted.

The musical director was casting, running through the script from the beginning, and auditioning the roles as they came up; you had a chance to audition for one, and you either got it or you didn't. It was like an elimination line as the characters appeared in the play.

I was chuffed that I got a part quite early on in the play, but realised afterwards that I had about four lines, and then what I assumed was the character fainting was actually her death. So I didn't have much of a speaking role in the play. I did, however, do some chorus parts as well. It was just so important for me to do activities outside of school, especially with people who had no association with my school or school life.

There was a lovely boy, Fionn, who was also in the play with me, with whom I had great fun and got on well. He was a kind boy who was comfortable being himself. There were a few house parties around the time of the end of the show. Fionn and I were both non-drinkers, but we both were up for a laugh. We would dance and chat and have great fun. At the time, I was actually going out with another guy, and Fionn was seeing a girl, so we were just good friends. We swapped numbers and kept in touch.

That summer of fifth (going into sixth) year, we met up and were both single, and so we started dating for a little while. It was difficult to meet up much, because I lived in the middle of nowhere, and he lived on the other side of Dublin. I was also doing my evening classes, some voluntary work, and extracurricular activities, and Fionn had a similarly full timetable with his activities and studies (he was hoping to study medicine). Around the end of September of sixth year, we had both decided that it was more of a friendship, and that we had to be practical about it. I still went to his school ball with him that December and we had brilliant night. And we remained good friends.

*

One Thursday afternoon after school when I was in sixth year, Mum picked me up from school and drove me across the city centre to the south of Dublin. I wasn't 100% sure what this trip would entail, but she explained that we were going to visit an expert in dyslexia whom she had found by fluke. She had opened up the yellow pages phone directory to look up people who did assessments on dyslexia, and his name had come up. He was actually a neuropsychologist. Mum explained to him a little bit about my situation, particularly around the fact that I have profound dyslexia and dyspraxia, and extreme difficulties with reading and writing, and was currently trying to get the provision of a reader and scribe sanctioned for my Leaving Cert (state examinations).

He then said to Mum that he would be very interested in meeting me and doing a bit of work with me. He was writing a book at the time, and wanted to put some case studies in, and he thought I could potentially be a good subject.

We turned up at his office, which was a prefab on the side of a house, and he invited us in. He was a tall man, with a big hairy beard. I felt apprehensive about suddenly going to somebody who was saying that potentially he could "fix" me. In addition, when we first got there, he was asking me lots of intimate questions about myself, and I felt uncomfortable.

He would say things like, "Oh, you don't have a good short-term memory. The only reason you can remember that is actually because you have attached it to an emotional memory."

I would get defensive and say, "No."

Some of it was because I didn't have the inside information to understand the neuro anatomy, but another reason was that I felt vulnerable: there was a person on the other side of the room whom I'd met only half an hour ago who could tell me lots of in-depth details about myself.

He insisted that this was the case. He then did an illustration: he told me, for example, that Mum's eyes go to this side when she is remembering things from the past and to the other side when she thinks about the future. He asked Mum to remember her First Communion, and her eyes did go in the direction that he told me they would. Following that, he asked Mum to think about what she was going to cook tomorrow, and a series of other questions, and each time he got it right and knew exactly where her eyes were going to go. At that stage, I gave up being protective and defensive, and openly chatted to him about my difficulties.

He spoke about different perspectives, and while I can't remember exactly how he did it, he determined that I have about five different perspectives in how I see things. Whether it's straight down, slightly looking up, looking to the left or right, it varies and can affect how I perceive or receive information. This also made sense; as a little girl I used to sit and tell my mum that I had to go into a big tunnel to try to read, and even then I would be so exhausted after getting into this tunnel that I wouldn't necessarily be able to retain or understand what I read.

Sometimes when I try to read, the words run around the page. But on top of that, I sometimes feel motion sickness – truly physically sick – when I try to read. His explanation about multiple perspectives made some sense of this.

He got me to do some handwriting tasks. When I focused on a certain point, my handwriting was slightly more legible. It was still heavy handed and not as evenly spaced, but the actual formation of the letters was a bit more symmetrical when I was looking down and up. He had me spell words backwards, and surprisingly (as I said before, I could do the alphabet backwards as a child) it was easier for me to spell words backwards.

He would write the word forwards in the first instance, showing me it, and then I would spell it out backwards. I was to visualise trying to space the letters of the word on the wall from one corner of the room to the other. He would point a laser on the wall at the point where I was meant to go next. He also got me to make shopping lists, listing 20 or 30 items, and have me repeat them back (which was training my short-term memory). He got me to think about sequences as well, such as a little animal coming round and sitting on a bigger animal, and then a bigger animal and a smaller animal, and then they all went home; this was to visualise different sequences of animals. He also sent me home with some exercises, which I had to practise every day but did require an adult to support me in doing the reading and writing tasks.

In some ways, part of me was anxious when he said he could potentially cure me. I had always been dyslexic; I always had difficulties with my reading and writing, and for someone to suddenly change who I was, my perspective, and my ability, was terrifying. I wondered, if I were fixed, would I still be HANNAH. Yes, I had always wondered what it would be like if only I didn't have dyslexia or dyspraxia. Now I was potentially faced with an opportunity where someone had the ability to give me the key to open that door, and that was both amazing and frightening.

I did all of these exercises regularly for a few weeks, and we went back. I was still struggling with my reading and spelling. Mum and I decided that the workload on both of us, and the hour and a half drive over to south Dublin wasn't practical on an ongoing basis. This time commitment was not feasible as I was going into my final year of school. In reality, these techniques were probably more about improving my concentration, sequencing, and memory, alongside trying to train my eye to read from left to right. Looking back now, these exercises were more aimed at improving these areas rather than "curing" the dyslexia.

*

When I was in sixth year, the final year of secondary school, I again had to have a psychological assessment. You needed to have one done within a certain timeframe and I was due an up-to-date assessment in order to get my exemption from Irish, and from spelling and grammar for my exams. It was very different doing this assessment as a 17-year-old than it was when I'd had my first assessment with Anne, where I had been oblivious to the point of the games she had me complete. Now I knew that these games led to labels. I knew when I was getting things wrong, and felt very frustrated with myself. But equally, when I got things right (especially with the sums and mathematical problems), I felt really excited and that I was doing well. In other parts I got very upset. I had to work hard not to have an emotional outburst; I was still triggered by being asked to read out loud, and I felt like I was back in The Teacher's class. This was picked up by the psychologist, who wrote: "*Hannah became quite upset when she struggled; however, Hannah has developed multiple techniques that help her compensate for these difficulties.*" She was able to identify these, for example, by my using my fingers as memory tools to remember letters or by visualising something. The report seemed to focus on the things that I found difficult and quantified them. It was probably the first time that I had seen my difficulties quantified.

Hearing and seeing that I had a reading age of seven-year-old or spelling age of an 11-year-old was quite shocking. I had thought that I had improved and was doing much better.

*

My great-aunt, Pearl, had a friend in New York, and when I was 18, Mum, Ruth, Pearl, and I went for a visit.

On the aeroplane over, I said to Pearl, "I hope it snows!" It wasn't meant to snow, but two days later it did. Pearl was in a wheelchair, which was very difficult to push in the snow, and she blamed me for wishing it on us, but I thought it was beautiful.

Outside Macy's, a man gave us fliers to go to a film premiere of *Mona Lisa Smile*, so Mum, Pearl, Ruth, and I all went down to the cinema where it was screened. There were loads of people there, and we ended up waiting for ages. Finally, we got chatting with an employee, and they said, "Oh no. Actually we only take 50 people from this queue. It's to make sure that all of the seats are full in the screening."

I can't remember the ins-and-outs of it, but we convinced the employee to give us two tickets to get in. Pearl and Mum decided that they would go and have a cup of tea, while Ruth and I saw the movie.

Pearl said, "You're young – you go."

We got a free popcorn and drink, and we went and sat in the seats that we had been allocated. There were loads of famous people there – Julia Roberts, Kirsten Dunst, and a couple of the other cast members stood up at the beginning of the screening and introduced the film. I imagined then that someday it would be my face on the screen, and I would be attending a premier of one of my movies. I had my dreams, and I was so motivated to work extra hard to ensure I got a place on a Performing Arts degree course.

*

I was due to sit my Leaving Cert in a few months but I was becoming very stressed that I would not do well. Part of the worry and fear was that I still had not been sanctioned by the Education Board to have a reader and scribe for my exams. It's funny because in Ireland at that time it was a lot easier to get a reader and scribe for your Junior Cert than it was for your Leaving Cert. Part of the reason is probably that there is a thing called Leaving Cert Applied, which is an alternative route to doing the Leaving Cert: it is less academic and more practical, and maybe they expect people who tend to need readers and scribes to go down the Leaving Cert Applied route as opposed to the traditional Leaving Cert.

I was having panic attacks, and wondering if all of the hours of work that I was putting in were worth it. Every part of my bedroom wall was covered in Art History paintings, and I would look at them and learn them. I would sleep with the books under my bed, hoping that osmosis would occur, and I would somehow know all of the information.

My whole life was focused on the Leaving Cert, as were my friends' lives. A lot of my friends were also aiming very high: some wanted straight As, and they had a lot of pressure on them. The added frustration for me was the fact that I wasn't sure I would be given the opportunity to allow myself to prove the stuff that I had learned and the work I had put in, and be validated for that work. I also knew that I had my place in my university in London, provided I got my grades, so that was quite stressful. A few times, my parents were called and asked to take me home because I would end up having an anxiety attack. I would go into the bathroom and try to contain my feelings, and would then cry and get really, really frustrated. I wouldn't be able to speak properly and would have to go home. An Irish teacher put Rescue Remedy in a big glass of water and told my parents they reckoned they should buy me a supply of it, or the Rescue Remedy gums.

One day, there was a school spiritual retreat. It was all about meditation and where we want to be in life. Sitting there, I had the time to reflect, and found myself thinking, *You know what? I'm not going to do this. I am going to give up because there's no point in – again – being told that I'm not good enough. If I don't play the game I won't get caught out. I don't have to fail.* I felt like I was being set up to fail. The retreat facilitator played a song which went, "I just can't give up now ..." and I felt overwhelmed, as if someone had given me the message that it's not okay to give up: don't lose faith, hold yourself together, and it's going to be okay. I went up to him afterwards and asked, "Who sang that song? Where can I get a copy?" I explained that I was really struggling, and that those words had given me the kick that I needed. He handed me the CD and said, "You need this CD. This is for you." I would listen to it regularly, singing along when I felt disheartened. To this day, it has been a recurring song for me. I just can't give up.

*

I was part of the student council from second year, when I was 14, to sixth year. We had vending machines installed in the school, and with the profit that was made from the machines, we bought picnic benches for the school's common areas. We also ran a mentoring programme and a couple of other little projects. We were the student representatives when it came to things for which the school wanted students' input.

Student council was made up of a couple of members from each year with different types of interests. Everyone involved did it for their own reasons. As part of the student council, we were invited to different conferences, one of which was the Union of Secondary School Students Annual Conference. I was in sixth year, my final year of school, when I went to one of their conferences. There were guest speakers and mini-projects. There was also an Education Officer, a PR Officer, a Finance Officer, Treasurer, and Chairperson, all of whom were members of other student councils.

On the first day of the conferences, we met outside Temple Bar. I was there with my friend Tom. Being quite extroverted, I went up to a group and said, "Hi! I'm Hannah!" Tom and I decided that it would be good fun to play Zip, Zap, Boing, an icebreaker game, with the group. Everyone was a willing participant and joined in. After we had done this silly little game, and everyone had gone around and introduced themselves, a dark-haired six-foot-something guy, wearing jeans and a black zip-up jumper, stepped forwards, and said, "Hi, I'm James and I'm leading this group." James was an Officer for the Union of Secondary School Students.

During the next two days of the conference, the board sat on the stage, and the debates, questions, and events that were on were introduced by different board members. I thought that James seemed really nice. He was quiet but had a presence about him. That evening, all the students stayed in hostels in the city centre. People were in different rooms, playing games and chatting. In one of the rooms, there was a sing-song. I was in the same room as James and we got chatting. After the conference, we swapped numbers and from then we started dating. We only saw each other on weekends, as James lived in South Dublin, whereas I lived in North Dublin.

James and I had different personalities: he was quiet and book smart, measured and organised, whereas I was much more scatty, emotional, and extroverted. But we both had strong ideas of who we were. James found school easy; he was very intelligent and an all-rounder (editor of the school paper, on the football team). When we met up on the weekends, we would often study together because we had our Leaving Cert coming up in June. James was the best study buddy. He would help me with my French, and he used to write me these crib sheets, which had key verbs and useful sentences in French. He did the same for me in English; if he read a study guide that had good quotes or sentences about Emily Dickinson or the other poets that we were studying, he would share it with me. When we weren't studying, we would also play chess and do crosswords together; I had never done a crossword before then, because obviously you had to be able read and spell words. But James would read the clues to me and we would do the crosswords together. He probably knew most of the answers prior to my guessing them, but it was fun to do together. James was so genuine; when I was with him, it was so easy. I was able to be me, things were simple, and I felt accepted.

That June, we both sat the Leaving Cert. I had accepted my place to go to university in London (subject to results), and James was planning on going to a university in Dublin. James and I hadn't discussed what was going to happen next. That July, I was working as a children's courier for a campsite in France. James came over to France to visit me and we camped for a week in Paris. While there, James and I climbed the Eiffel Tower. Paris looked beautiful, as the sun was starting to set, and it should have been very romantic. Instead, the uncertainty of whether we would manage to stay together when we went to university made me anxious: I asked James, "What's happening when I go to London?"

James said, "Well, we're so young, and London is far away … I'm not sure the long-distance thing will work, so we will probably just have to break up when you go." I understood his logic, but it felt foreboding knowing that an end was coming. It seemed like I was investing in something that was about to expire. I asked if we could just break up now. He understood why I felt that way. So, we decided we were breaking up on the Eiffel Tower, but we promised that we would stay good friends.

A few weeks later, our Leaving Cert exam results came out. When I saw my points, I cried my eyes out. Even though I had got enough for university and had done quite well, I didn't score as highly as I had on the mock exams. Tom got the maximum 600 points, James got 590; everyone was getting A1s and I didn't quite score the same. I got one A and a few Bs and Cs, and just didn't feel as happy with myself. I had called James to let him know my results and he could tell that I wasn't too pleased. That night when I met up with him, he handed me a A4 page. He had written statistics showing me that my grades were in the top 10% and most students who get these results do this course, etc. It made me feel much happier about myself and my results, and I was able to celebrate fully.

In my first year of university, I went home to Dublin for the Easter midterm break. While I was back, I met up with James, and he showed me how to structure an essay properly. My next coursework submission was the first essay that I got an A on in university. James knew nothing about Performing Arts; he once said, "All I know about acting is what I've watched on *Friends*, and Joey seemed to have a lot of free time on his hands." So, he didn't do the work for me, but he was very good at facilitating my needs and giving me nuggets of information, like how to structure an academic essay (introduction, four points, conclusion, conflicting quotes, references, etc.). I am really lucky that James came into my life when he did.

Cedarwood Close 1987

Me and Jenny

The day Killian arrived

Teenage years

National Lifesaving Champions

Chapter Three: University

The future belongs to those who believe in the beauty of their dreams.

- *Eleanor Roosevelt*

Getting a degree and going to college was always very important to me. It was what happened in the movies and it was part of my life plan. I never realized how supported I had been until I had to navigate the *real world* on my own. I also learnt the extent of my difficulties, motivation, and determination during these years.

Early one Monday morning, Mum and I sat in Dublin airport waiting to board a Ryanair flight. I talked Mum's ear off on the way, telling her about my wonderful apartment and planning all of the things that we were going to do in London, including shopping on Oxford Street.

At Luton Airport, Mum and I got the coach into London. The coach drove past Marble Arch and Hyde Park, where I squeezed Mum's arm and said, "Oh! This is where *101 Dalmatians* was shot!" Mum and I got off the coach and I gathered all of my belongings, including a sunflower poster. We got off the bus at Victoria Coach Station and crossed over the road to get the tube to Holloway Road Tube Station. At the station exit there was a sign. I asked Mum what the large sign said, and she read it out to me. It was about a shooting that had occurred the previous day on Holloway Road, calling for any witnesses to the murder. I suddenly felt a little bit afraid; this was not how I'd imagined the beginning of my life-to-be, as an independent young adult, living in London.

As we walked down Holloway Road, I still felt that nervous anticipation as I dragged my heavy suitcases behind me, not quite sure how far away my apartment was from the tube station. I was so excited when I left the tube station, because I saw the large university buildings opposite the tube, and remembered the excitement of my audition to get into the university. I couldn't believe that they actually wanted me, and that I was going to get a degree, and I would be an actress! As we walked down Holloway Road looking for the new apartment blocks of student accommodation, I spotted the big red pub, and the carpet shop, and then the apartment blocks above. Mum helped me complete the forms and hand over any necessary cheques, and we were given a set of keys. In the lift on the way up, we squeezed in with a girl called Penny, who had a large shopping trolley filled with bright pink fluffy things and a large television. I only had two suitcases with me. Mum and I had intended on buying a duvet and some pillows in London, as it was less expensive than buying them at home and paying for extra luggage.

I could not wait to meet the new friends that I was going to be living with. When I opened the door, though, it smelled like cigarette smoke and I was very disappointed, as I had specifically asked to be in a non-smoking apartment. My bedroom was not like it looked in the brochures or on the internet. The stained carpet was scratchy and grey. The walls had four or five different colours of paint on them. The drip of the tap in the sink was getting to me, and the stains on the mattress were upsetting, and I could see the springs poking through. I have always had very weird issues about cleanliness, and my space, and my room and my bed have always been very important to me. I am also incredibly sensitive to noise, and the dripping of the tap was going to drive me mad.

"This is not how it is meant to be!" I cried to Mum, who had sat down on the bed. "This is not how it is meant to be!"

We went to look at the sitting room, only to find that it was a shared kitchen with four moulded plastic chairs, a table, a large fridge, no washing machine, and a stained floor. An Italian girl, an Austrian girl, and an English girl, whose room smelled like marijuana, came into the kitchen with their bags and were putting away food and drinks in the fridge, and placing pots and pans away all in the communal area. These girls were all older than me and none of them had their mothers with them. They all seemed to know what this shared accommodation living was all about, and just got on with it. I asked them if they were disappointed with their bedrooms, and they said, "Uh, a little bit. It's a bit small." Nobody mentioned the cleanliness or the colours of the wall. Mum and I went down to reception and tried to swap for a different apartment, but because the university year had just started, all of the rooms had been allocated to other students, so we decided that we would have to make the most of the room that I was given. Mum suggested that we could paint the wall. We sought permission from the management, and were allowed to paint the wall as long as it was cream or white. We spent two days painting. We purchased a mattress protector from Argos along with some new duvets and pillows, and I hung up my poster of a bright yellow sunflower where the marks on the wall had been. Maintenance came up and fixed the leaking tap, so I felt a little bit happier about my new apartment.

Mum and I did not spend a day shopping on Oxford Street; we were exhausted by the evening and still had no plates, pots, or pans. We walked down the street and found a 99p store. We saw that they were selling pots, plates, and cups. Mum and I were so excited that everything was only 99p. In Ireland, we have a similar shop called the Pound Shop where nothing is £1. Certainly not brand names. Mum was in one aisle and I was in the other, saying, "Oh! This is only 99p!" and, "Mum, this is only 99p!" It didn't take long until our baskets were filled to the brim.

As Mum said, "And this is only 99p!" an Irish voice said,

"Oh, the joys of an Irish person finding a 99p store." At this, we giggled and turned around to see a petite lady in her early 20s. "Hi, I'm Aoife," she said, and asked us where we were moving in with the large baskets of belongings. We explained that I had just begun university and had moved into the arcade on Holloway Road.

"Ah, I know it well. A bit of a dive," she said.

"Yes!" I exclaimed.

We asked her how she knew it and she explained that she had studied a PGDip in Education there the previous year. They had also apparently nicknamed it "The Prison", which makes a lot of sense. Aoife gave me her number and said that if I fancied having a cup of tea with proper teabags to give her a shout, and that she was only living up the road in a house with some friends. Aoife was a primary school teacher and seemed safe enough. I did not intend on ever calling her, though. I left the 99p store and returned to my apartment block with my new delph and cutlery. I decided that I would store the delph in my own closet in my bedroom, as I was not really into the whole sharing thing yet.

Two days later, Mum was still in London and I had to register for my courses. I approached the university with my passport, my offer of a place, and my grades. I had queued in the wrong building; they had separated Arts and Humanities. I found the right building, where were more than 100 other people all trying to register. I did not realise that there was a ticketing system, and had been waiting a long time before I went up and asked. My stress levels were mounting: I was feeling frustrated and had no awareness of how long this was going to take. I had not bought a mobile phone yet, and was unable to tell Mum that I was going to be longer than expected. I eventually reached the front of the queue where we were handed login details, and told to go and register on the computers. I got very upset and explained that I would need some support with this. There was one gentleman who was receptive to my needs, and he came over and helped me to fill in my details on the form on the computer. He then said, "Hey, you don't have to queue again for the photo – I will just take it now." I had big red eyes from crying, so my photo looked horrendous. When I was handed my student card, I asked what would happen if I lost my card. I was told, "Don't worry. We still have your photo on the system for the next few years." I remembered now what my friends had told me before starting university – that the photo is very important. I had already failed at this. Suddenly, my dreams and expectations of what university life was going to be like started to feel very uncertain.

The next day of university was the first day of induction. We were all handed module course outlines, big large documents of sheets and reams of writing. Mum left London that morning. I went to my accommodation with my new paperwork, left it on the desk, and thought no more of it. I had looked at my timetable and was aware that I needed to be in at 9:30am. When I attended my first lecture, apart from getting lost again and being in the wrong building, and turning up to class late and fretting, I sat down on the floor and we all started discussing a play. I thought it was interesting that everyone must have read this play for their A levels, like I had read *Macbeth* for my Irish Leaving Certificate. But then they started to discuss the characters in more depth and applying theory to the text. I was asked my opinion, and I told them I could not comment – that I had not actually read it. That's when I found out we were meant to have read this play before the first session, which had been in the course handout.

When I finally got home after my first real day at university, I was still feeling stressed out about not being the same as the rest of the students, and afraid I was not going to be able to make it through the first week without some support. I tried to ring Mum to tell her about what had happened, but I could not get through. I scrolled down my new mobile phone, which had about four phone numbers in it, one of which was Aoife's, the girl I had met in the 99p store. I gave her a call and said that I would love to pop over for a cup of tea. When I came over, I explained what had happened in class, and I brought the module outline with me. She sat down, went through it, and wrote a letter to the university Disability Team on my behalf, making a formal complaint that I had not received any support, nor had any accessible or reasonable adjustments been made. I dropped this letter in to the Disability Support Centre at the university and got chatting to the receptionist. The Disability Officer came out and explained that, although other students have support, I was falling between two stools. As I was an Irish student studying in England, my funding came from Ireland, and this would take a while to come through and be sanctioned. In the meantime, I was told to just try to keep up the best I could.

That evening, I called Aoife and told her what the university had said. She offered to come over to my apartment and read through the module outline for me. I taped her reading the module outline, and colour coded all of the different sections, noting the deadlines for each week. I bought a calendar and she wrote the essay deadlines on my calendar. I rang Mum and asked if she could do some reading for me as she had often done in the past. Mum also bought copies of the plays that I was meant to read, and would record them on cassette tapes and post them over to me tape by tape. My ex-boyfriend, James, was very supportive, too, and would often help by spell-checking my emails, as would Aoife.

The university had organised for me to liaise with the Volunteer Reading Group, which was generally for people who wanted to do some voluntary work reading to the elderly. This service was offered to me for a couple of hours here and there. For instance, I might have half an hour during the day where I would go and have someone read to me. The people who would read to me, however, were not necessarily very skilled in reading, for example, pronouncing the words "oral" and "aural" the same, which confused me, especially for my speech course books. One of the ladies also had a high-pitched voice that whistled; I found it difficult to process any information that she was saying, so I had to ask her to speak in a deeper voice, which I think she found a bit strange.

*

I had a German dance teacher, Yannik, who was also a lecturer in Performing Arts. Yannik was passionate about the arts. In his dance class, which we all had to take as part of the Performing Arts degree, I used to knock into other students regularly. Again, my wrong foot would come out and my body positions and ability to isolate individual movements was poor.

Yannik asked me to come to his office one day because he was going to do some individual work with me. Yannik used lots of Laban and Feldenkrais techniques in his classes, which are styles of movement based on dance and therapy. I came into his office unsure what to expect to do in such a small space. He put his hands on my hips, and then he got me to go down on the floor. He started pulling my legs forwards and backwards, getting me to crawl like a baby. I thought this was really weird, and he used to say stuff like, "Move your hips – ja!" I had never really moved that way before and I felt a bit silly, but I also felt safe, as Yannik was a kind and passionate teacher. I think he knew I would never be a dancer, but he wanted to help me enjoy the art of movement. I came to his office three more times, doing the same type of crawling patterns. Crawling is the first developmental milestone that I'd never met as a baby. So, at 19 years old, I learnt to crawl with the help of Yannik. And surprisingly enough, I believe it actually helped improve my coordination and body scheming greatly.

On another occasion, I handed in a draft of an essay to Yannik; it was typed but was just lots of words, so it was a bit "gobbledegook", but we had to hand in a draft. My support worker hadn't had a chance to type it up for me at that stage; it was just my ideas. I handed it in, and after class one day, he said to me, "Hannah, this is amazing. It's like a piece of art."

I said, "Oh, did you like it? Could you read it?"

Yannik said, "Oh, no no. Just the way that you write words, and the letters that you put together: the combinations are just beautiful. It's like a picture! It's art!" He was eccentric, but he seemed to have seen the beauty in my difficulties, and could appreciate the beauty in being a little bit different.

*

I loved going out. They had a nightclub called Big Fish, which was in walking distance of the dormitory, and where we could just dance. One friend I'd made in my first year living in London was a professional salsa dancer. He had offered to teach me and Gabriela, my Italian flatmate, how to salsa dance, and we would make dinner for him in exchange. I loved the idea of being able to do salsa dancing. I was confident, and with the right teacher I could learn just like in the movies! I am hypermobile, which usually is not a good thing when trying to sit up straight, but for fancy salsa moves, being flexible is an advantage! I was very good at doing the bendy back move and whipping up, but as for the basic steps, I could just not get them. I kept jumping up and down like an Irish dancer doing one, two, threes. "It's all in the hips," he kept saying. So I tried that, but then I wasn't moving my feet enough. I was not very good at being led, and kept doing whole body movements. Gabriela had a much better sense of rhythm. After a handful of sessions, we decided I had probably learnt as much as I could without having mastered the basics!

*

I needed to get a part-time job, so I handed my CVs out all over Covent Garden because that is where I had always wanted to work. It was part of my plan, my dream – my favourite place in London.

There was a little shop that sold hand and beauty products. I was interviewed and offered a part-time job there until Christmas. I did not have a bank account at this stage, and this was important in order to be paid. I worked for two weeks in the shop and was told that if I did not get a bank account, they would have to let me go, as they weren't able to pay me.

I went into the local bank and asked them for the form to open a bank account. I took the form home and had a friend help me complete it. I came back to the bank for the appointment that had been arranged to open my account. As I sat down, I handed the bank employee my form and my passport.

"Oh!" she said. "You are not a UK citizen. You have filled in the wrong form." Ripping my form in half and placing it in the bin, she took out a new form, handed it to me, and asked me to fill it in.

I explained, a little bit embarrassed and anxious at this stage, "Oh, I'm sorry. You see, I have dyslexia and dyspraxia, and I have difficulties filling in forms. That's why I had the other one pre-filled in. I'm wondering, could you please help me?"

She said, "No problem", and began to ask me questions:

"What is your post code?"

"How do you spell … ?"

I said, "I don't know how to spell that, but I do know it's correctly spelled on the other form. Perhaps you could just copy the details from the other form?"

To this, she replied, "Oh! No! You are too clever to be dyslexic."

I felt really rubbish. I was embarrassed and annoyed, especially as she started to giggle. I then smiled and laughed with her, swallowing my pride and my sense of "this is so wrong".

She helped me fill in the form and I left the bank. A few days later, I received my card and pin in the post. I had mixed feelings about this. Although I had successfully opened a bank account, I had been given the impression that people with dyslexia were not considered intelligent. In hindsight, I should have corrected her.

*

Some classmates of mine decided that we would form a study group. One of the girls would sit and read to me and I would explain the contents of the book. I often grasped things pretty quickly, and was fast with processing once I could access the material. My personal tutor had also organised for me to listen to recordings of some of the plays, which had been kept in the archives of a large central library. I was excited about this, and finally felt that I was at a point where I was keeping on top of things and understanding what it was all about. I approached the library with my letter from the university saying that I had an appointment and was a student studying in London. It was enormous, like something from Ancient Rome – big, marble-y, echo-y. There were lots of people in the foyer. I approached a desk with my letter.

The librarian said, "No problem." The tape had been retrieved from the archives and a room had been booked, as had been mentioned by my tutor, but first I needed to become a member and complete a form.

I asked them to help me to complete the form, giving my usual explanation about my difficulty in filling out forms. The librarian said that it was not their policy to help people to fill in these forms and that I needed to do it myself. "You should have written to us to tell us you were coming and needed help to fill in the form," she said. "Then we could have made arrangements for this."

"If I were able to write such a letter," I replied, "then I wouldn't need or be asking for help and I wouldn't have this problem!"

I felt panicky. I looked at my watch: I had less than ten minutes before I was due to listen to this recording. The recording of the play took two hours and the library would be closing at six o'clock, so I needed to make sure that I got in and couldn't be delayed. Not knowing the ending of a play would have been a really bad move.

I approached a group and asked if they would help. They were tourists and said that they didn't speak good English, and that they were just taking photos. I then found another guy who was sitting in the corner; I smiled nicely at him. Although I was slightly uncomfortable and he was a complete stranger, I asked him to help fill in the form. The form asked for lots of personal details, like my address, date of birth, and phone number, and I gave all of these freely to this man. I had a sheet of stickers which had my name, address, phone number and national insurance number printed on them. Mum had made me these when I moved over so I could stick them on things. I showed these to him.

Thinking about it now, I was very lucky he wasn't a weirdo. I was quite naïve and vulnerable as a 19-year-old in London, living on my own.

I got into the alcoves and listened to the whole play. The first 10 or 20 minutes, though, had been wasted. My heart was pounding, I was sweaty, and I just felt that nothing was going to be easy. As soon as I felt that I was in control, I would get another knock.

I also joined the local library and found the section where they had audiobooks. I selected some audiobooks to listen to that were relevant to my coursework and some just for leisure. I tried to take them out and was told that there would be a charge of £1.50 per cassette. I asked why this was, to which I was given the response: "Because there are fewer audio books available in the library and therefore they have a charge."

I explained that I was dyslexic and unable to read the other books, and the whole point of the library is for people to access knowledge regardless of their income. The librarian said that that was not their library's policy, and if I would like to make a complaint about it, I should fill in a complaint form.

I said that I would like to make a complaint about this, and would she please assist me to fill in the form, as I have dyslexia, hence why I needed the audio books. She said "no problem" and helped me to fill in the form. I stressed in the form that I have difficulty accessing the written word, and therefore need materials in alternative formats.

Two weeks later, I received a letter in the post, which my flatmate read to me:

Their response was something along the lines of *Thank you very much for your suggestion, but at this point in time we are not going to consider it.*

How ironic that not only had they missed the purpose of their library, but they had also not taken any notice of the fact that the written word is not accessible to me and potentially to other patrons wishing to access their services.

Luckily, my support funding finally came through around Christmas, which meant more regular access to my supports.

*

When I was little, I struggled to use a knife and fork, and would often use my hands. My mum sometimes said that the way I ate would make her feel sick: spilling the food everywhere and getting it under my nails. If I did try to use a fork or a spoon, I would literally shovel it into my mouth, using a primitive whole-hand grasp. I would dislike using utensils, because it felt uncomfortable. I would be propping myself up on the table with one elbow, trying to coordinate the movement of getting food onto the spoon and into my mouth. I also found cutting and slicing pieces of meat very difficult, so it was easier if I just picked it up with my hand. Whenever I had friends over, I would always ask Mum for burgers, pizzas, or chips – anything I could eat with my hands. I managed to get by this way until I was about 18. By this time, I was obviously able to hold a spoon or a fork, but was still shovelling food into my mouth, and frankly, it was quite grotesque.

At university, I had a boyfriend, Matt, who was quite "cultured". He was older than me at 24 years old. He once took me to a restaurant, and I think he was horrified when he saw how I ate.

"You can't eat like that!" he said.

I didn't see the problem with the way I was eating, but did become a bit embarrassed when he said this, and turned bright red.

"I don't know how to eat any other way," I told him.

"Well," he said, "I will teach you."

When I had first tried to learn how to use a knife and fork, I was also struggling to hold a pencil, to tie a shoelace, to ride a bike, to sit still. There were so many other skills that needed to come into place long before I was able to master the skills of using a knife and fork. I still had difficulty with gauging pressure, which caused a lot of difficulty with cutting: I could try to stick the fork down, and use the knife, but my hand ended up slipping because I was too firm with the knife on the plate. As a young adult, I was highly motivated, and embarrassed that somebody I was trying to impress would be so disgusted by the way I ate, that they would not want to be seen in social situations with me. By not having the skills, I felt I would be isolated. So Matt taught me to use a knife and fork.

One day, he came to my apartment, put the knife and fork where they needed to be, and said, "If you are eating spaghetti, you use a spoon and hold the fork this way. This is how you put the fork into your mouth: you don't shove it; you stop it midway; and you turn the fork and direct it into your mouth. And you have to eat slower."

I did find, actually, that when I would go to restaurants with Matt, I was aware that he was very tuned in to how I ate. I would pick something on the menu that was really simple and didn't require much cutting, or which would stay on the spoon or fork easily. So I learned how to use a knife and fork properly when I was 18, going on 19.

I don't know if I would have been able to master those skills as a child. I did have some input when I was younger. Killian had an occupational therapist as part of his service, and my mum mentioned to her that I was struggling with using a knife and fork.

I was given what I now know is "caring cutlery", a fork with lots of ridges. Mine was orange. But I didn't have any spoons or knives. I was also unable to tie my shoelaces, and was really struggling. Again, the OT gave Mum this big toy shoe, and I would have to practise on that. I would also practise on teddy bears, and we would tie ribbons. By the time I was 14, I had definitely mastered this skill as I got a job working in a Belgian chocolate mini-factory, where I was hired to tie all the bows on the chocolates!

Matt had a coffee pod machine in his college dorm room. He had childhood friends visiting for the weekend, and they had spent the day at the Tower of London looking at the Crown Jewels while I worked at my little shop in Covent Garden. At the end of the day, Matt picked up some stuff to make a pasta dinner, and his friends picked up some chocolate cake for dessert.

After dinner, we took out Monopoly to play while drinking coffee and eating dessert. I was exhausted, as I had just worked a full day, and drank my coffee quickly. During the game of Monopoly, my cheeks became really red, and my speech became quite pressured. I was not aware of other people's boundaries, and my limbs were going everywhere – and so was the chocolate cake.

At the end of the evening, Matt said that he felt embarrassed by my giddy behaviour and suggested that I should maybe not drink coffee.

Another evening, around the same time as the coffee and chocolate cake incident, I had been out working all day in Covent Garden, and a housemate of mine invited me out dancing with her and her other friends. The housemate I lived with at the time was at least 12 years older than me, so I had not met or socialised with a lot of her friends before.

As we headed to the nightclub, I said, "Oh, I'm feeling really tired after a long day of working."

A little bit later, I was on the dancefloor throwing lots of shapes, excited and giddy and being really social.

One of the girls said, "Oh, you've recovered well!"

I said, "Oh yeah! Don't worry – I've just had some Coke."

About half an hour later, I was invited to the toilet by one of the girls. I thought it was like the way girls go off to the toilet together sometimes, and I said "Yeah!" *Lovely*, I thought, *they are being friendly!*

When I got into the stall with her, I was invited to do a line of cocaine.

I freaked out and said, "No! God no!", and left.

She followed me out, saying, "But I thought you had said you had some coke?"

"No," I said, "I meant Coca-Cola!"

Earlier that evening, the woman, who was a director, had been doing a rendition of *King Lear* and had said I would be perfect to audition for Cordelia. Following my outburst of "God no!" at her, needless to say she did not interact or socialise with me again, and I never did get a call to audition for Cordelia.

I now understand that I am easily stimulated by sugar and coffee, and that this makes me less aware of other people's boundaries. It makes me giddy, my cheeks go quite rosy, and I may present as though I have difficulties listening and focusing. It doesn't leave me in a favourable light with others. I'm really lucky that I actually love drinking water. I drink a huge amount of water, and it is something that I have done since I was very young. I always have a glass of water by my bedside, and it helps me feel calm. If I have a headache or am trying to concentrate, drinking water enables me to focus, as it does for many others, but I drink a ridiculous amount of water. To this day, I avoid caffeine, sugary drinks, and eating too much chocolate.

*

I loved being an adult and living in London, even if I did get it a bit wrong sometimes. Now I was on to my next ambition to be in the Rose of Tralee. I phoned up and asked all about the Rose of Tralee competition, finding out how to enter the London selection. I got a friend to help me with the forms and found a sponsor. I was invited to the first round of heats, and as there weren't that many of us, almost all of us got through to the final. In the end, I wasn't selected to be the London representative in Tralee. I was really disappointed because I wanted to go to the Dome in Kerry and be in the competition. But I told myself that it wasn't my turn yet, and I parked that dream.

*

In my first year of university, after I had broken up with Matt, I had a lot of free time on my hands. One day I was chatting to my Italian flatmate, Gabriella, in her room and moaning about something; she was meant to be writing her dissertation, but her friend Luigi came online and wanted to chat to her.

She said, "Here – you talk to him!"

So we started chatting a lot on Skype and MSN for hours at a time for several weeks. As it happened, that summer my family was going to Italy, and I joined them in the camper van for

111

part of their trip. Luigi drove down from where he lived, to Lake Garda to meet me in person for the first time.

We went on this really sweet, romantic date around Lake Garda, going for pizza and gelato, and driving around in his little Italian car. It was great fun, and when he dropped me off at the campsite, he told me he felt so sad! He was just like a typical Italian romantic hero from a film – a very good-looking, chiselled man. He said I was special and that there was an Italian expression which, for him, captured my outlook. This expression, he translated as "Luck helps the brave".

Luigi kept in touch and invited himself to visit us in Ireland at the end of the summer before I went back to university. I think he might have even booked his flights before I had asked my parents whether or not he could come.

Mum said, "Yes, of course! It's fine!" but Dad was a bit dubious of him.

"Where is he going to sleep?" he said, because our family house is quite small and we don't have any spare rooms.

"I don't know," I said. "I'll put a tent up for him."

Luigi came over with a lovely coffee pot for my mum; in Italy, you mind your mummy, and he didn't realise that it was my dad whom he needed to keep sweet rather than my mum. We pitched his tent in the garden. Luigi had brought his pyjamas with him, which were long, clingy, fitted fabric long-john-type pyjamas. In the morning, he would come into the house in his pyjamas and have breakfast with my family and me. I think he was very cold in the tent, and the dogs were circling the tent barking at night, and he couldn't sleep properly, so he got upgraded to my dad's camper van. It might also have been that, as I said, there wasn't much space in the house, and Dad said he didn't want us getting up to mischief.

I showed Luigi around Dublin, and on one of the days I had arranged to take Killian to the zoo. So Killian, Luigi, and I went to the zoo, which again probably wasn't his idea of a romantic day; Luigi returned home and our brief holiday romance ended there. But his *Luck helps the brave* became a mantra for me, particularly during challenging times.

*

I found out in university that there were opportunities for students to study in America, and one of my flatmates was looking into it, too. I decided that I would go along with her to the seminar about it. It was called a "semester abroad", and there were a couple of universities that were affiliated with ours. I started talking about it to some of my peers and some students in the years above us in the Performing Arts degree, and was told that nobody from the Performing Arts degree had ever been allowed to go abroad because the course is so different.

I thought, *Well, where does it say that? How come a performing arts student can't go?*

I went to my Year Head, who was also the Course Director, and said, "I really want to go to New York. How can I make this happen? What would I need to do?"

He said he thought it was a wonderful idea. His only concerns were whether I was strong enough academically, as generally you need to have a minimum of a B in the first year of your degree to be able to sustain and catch up on the work that you might have missed because you would be doing a different curriculum. I told him I would study extra hard, and I got my Bs and my As, and applied for the semester abroad. I was apparently the first Performing Arts student to actually be allowed to do a semester abroad. One good thing about always being left out was that it has taught me to question, knock on doors, work extra hard, and keep trying. This might have motivated me to try harder academically in my first year than my peers, and to achieve my high grades.

That summer before I went to America, I was back in Dublin on a night out in a bar in the city centre and bumped into Fionn, who was now studying medicine at Trinity. We chatted briefly, but I was heading to a different bar and he had just arrived. The next day, I sent him a text and didn't get a reply. That night, I got a phone call from my friend Niamh. She called to say that Fionn had died.

I was aware that Fionn had some heart difficulties, which was why he didn't play rugby. But when I'd spoken to him a few months before, he'd told me he had just been over to England to have it checked and all seemed fine. But obviously it wasn't. This sudden loss was terribly traumatic. I couldn't understand how a healthy person who didn't drink, smoke, or do drugs could die so suddenly. He was such a happy-go-lucky, genuinely lovely guy, who was always volunteering, and who was studying medicine. Why did he have to die? It just didn't make sense. After Fionn died, I was determined not to take life for granted, but to try live life a little bit more now for Fionn.

A few weeks later, I travelled to upstate New York for my semester abroad. I was studying musical theatre, and one of the modules I took was American musical theatre studies. The teacher began the module by giving everyone the same song to sing and act. He directed us to think about a loved one who had passed or who had broken up with you; the performance was to be about missing someone who had died or who was no longer in your life. We were told to bring in something to help us tell the story. I had a picture of Fionn and me from his graduation ball in secondary school, which I brought as my prop. In the middle of my performance, I broke down, so much so that the teacher pulled me aside and asked if everything was okay. I explained that the person whom I was performing about had actually just died six weeks before.

"It's good to use real memories," he told me, "but you also have to take responsibility and decide whether it's still too raw." He suggested that perhaps, because I was away from home, and because I didn't have a strong network of support (since I had just moved over); it would be good for me to speak to the counsellor.

It was my first time ever going to counselling. The counsellor was a lovely older man. We just chatted about Fionn for the first week, and bereavement in general, because my paternal grandmother had also died that summer. I wasn't very close to her at all, and she wasn't the most loving or supportive grandmother. The last thing she said to me was, "Oh, Hannah, you've put weight on." We discussed how I felt, and that I was upset and disappointed that I hadn't actually had a close relationship with her.

We started talking about my self-esteem, and the other people in my life who had roles that were significant but didn't necessarily fulfil them or hadn't been the most positive. For example, we ended up talking about The Teacher and those dreadful two years in that class, and how I had subconsciously continued an internal dialogue that would regularly play in my head, telling me that I wasn't good enough and that I was stupid. I don't think I'd ever questioned these internal beliefs and fears before. It was only by chatting with the counsellor that I became aware of these things I'd buried. Some of the counsellor's observations were that I clearly was not stupid, and that I was "an intelligent and well-adjusted young lady with great insight". He also asked if I would consider recording (whether writing or doing a tape recording) what I would like to say to The Teacher and the dead grandmother, telling them what I didn't get to say. I think this is really important, because in life we don't always get to address the things that we want to address at the time. As a child, I wasn't able to address or explore the issues, but now it was important that I got some closure and stood up for the eight-year-old me.

The health and wellbeing services and sporting amenities at that university were excellent. There were also many differences to my university in London. The support that I received involved paying another student in my class to write notes on carbon paper, which was provided to them. They got paid something like seven or eight dollars an hour, and they were attending the class anyway, so it made no difference to them. The note-taker would give me the notes immediately after class; I got the top sheet and they would keep the copy. The university also had support workers you could drop in on, who would help you with your essays, or with spell-checking, or typing of work.

I found that the university was a very different pace to what I was expecting, and to what I was used to in London. In the

States, it was one big student village, with campuses set up with students needs in mind. In some ways, it was like a bubble and a lot more sheltered, so that made things easier. Prior to commencing my studies, we got the reading lists, and we used my support fund to record actors reading some of the texts and key chapters, so that I could listen to them and keep on top of my workload. Me being me, as soon as I got the recording, I listened to it, so I had an understanding of the work prior to commencing the class. This made it easier for me to follow and retain the information I was being told.

When I was in the States, I got glandular fever or "mono" as they call it. Again, the university nurse was fantastic and took my bloods to confirm why I was so sick and prescribed me medication. I was bedbound for a few weeks, as I was quite poorly. When I was better, I made up for the time that I had lost and did a lot of travelling, going to everything that was on offer. I went to see musicals, ice-hockey games, and visited friends of friends, cousins, and other relations. I was even invited to the Hamptons for Thanksgiving. In short, I embraced the American experience.

My strong work ethic was acknowledged in the work I was producing, and I made the Dean's Honours List for my grades. I was adamant I wasn't going to take life for granted and that I was really living for Fionn. I loved my time in America and got very involved with different groups and societies. I was the Vice President of the Global Ambassador Society, a society which was comprised mainly of International Students. We arranged events that focussed on celebrating cultural diversity and also created opportunities for trips. I organised a society trip to Niagara Falls in Canada, which was just like the movies. As an international student on a semester abroad, I, along with the other international students, received invitations to a lot of extra events. We were invited to the University President's house for dinner, a special Christmas party in the Alumni house, and a lot of other events.

I was actually the only Irish student, so when there were things that were different about me, my fellow students just said it was because I was "Miss Ireland", or stated, "You Europeans are so profound." I remember one lady remarking, "You guys drive on the wrong side of the road," to which I said, "It's not the wrong side of the road. It's just a different side of the road."

My time in the States gave me much more of an understanding of who I was. I learned a lot about my own Irish culture and also about myself. It was only when I was placed in different environments, with different people (who didn't know me as the girl who couldn't read, or the girl who split her head open, or the girl who everybody hates) that people got to know me as a person who was confident and different. They were excited to learn from me.

I was living with the older students in the campus accommodation. There was one lovely girl who had studied at my university in London the previous year, and who had a connection to Ireland. She was studying to be a teacher for children with disabilities and was in her final year. She had a car and decided that we would go on a road trip to Philadelphia, where her cousin lived. We had a wonderful time, going out dancing and for dinners, and meeting lots of different people.

Her cousin worked for Fox News, and we got to sit behind the desk and read the news (or make up the news in my case), and it was really fun. That evening, we went for dinner with some friends of hers who, again, were lovely. They were of Polish background originally.

We were chatting and I made some facial expression, and, out of nowhere, one of the friends said, "I'd love to shoot you."

"Oh, I'm sorry – did I offend you or something?"

She laughed and replied, "No, I'm a photographer!" and handed me her card. "But honestly, you have a really interesting facial expressions and I would love to shoot you."

"Great," I said, "that sounds fun. I would love to." But I didn't think much more of it. When I returned to New York, I looked up the website on her card and, flicking through her portfolio, and I could see that she was quite a talented photographer.

So, with the help of my flatmate, I sent her a short email which led to calls to and fro, and we arranged a date to do a photoshoot. I went back to Philadelphia on a Greyhound bus a few weeks later and did the photoshoot with her. She put me up in her home, and it was all a bit surreal but a really exciting experience. It was a long day, and when I look at the photos now, it barely looks like me because she had curled my hair and used a lot of atmospheric lighting. It was something I had not done before, but I really enjoyed modelling.

There was another guy in America who was volunteering as a soccer coach at the university, so he wasn't a real student. He was also a photographer, mainly a sports photographer. I had become friendly with him because he was doing some evening classes that I was also taking. One day, we went to a Pumpkin Festival that was held in the local village. There was a John Deere tractor, hay bales, lots of pumpkins and autumn decorations. I was wearing a pair of ripped jeans, and he had a cowboy hat. I sat on a hay bale in front of the tractor, and he said "Wait", held his camera up to his eyes, and snapped. He then gave me his hat and we spontaneously created some scenes. After the festival, he printed some photos and gave them to me, saying, "Look, these are amazing. You should really get into modelling."

While studying in America, I could take extracurricular classes, for which I received extra credits. One of the classes I joined was Gospel Choir, because it sounded like it could be a bit of fun. One of my neighbours who lived in the same apartment block as me was doing it as well, so I went along.

We learned some songs, and there was a lot of clapping of hands, and we would wear robes when we performed. I was so bad at keeping the rhythm. I found it difficult to clap in time; I can clap, just not in a very coordinated or rhythmical way.

One of the girls linked her elbow to mine, pulling me from side to side and trying to tell me when to clap. In the end, we decided that maybe it would be better if I didn't physically clap, and just went side to side doing the hand gesture.

In December 2005, I was flying back from New York, having studied and lived there for the previous five months. I took an Aer Lingus flight back to Dublin to see my family before going back to university in London. I sat beside a man named Ben who was a tradesman in his 30's from northern England. He had been separated from his group of friends because they'd got to the airport late. I offered him a sweet as the plane took off and we began chatting. I told him that I had been in America, and all about my adventure. I even took my laptop out to show him photographs of my bedroom, the big American college football rivalry match and Niagara Falls. He listened to all of my stories, and I nosily asked him all about himself, his family, what he did, and whether he liked it. The seven hours ended up flying by (excuse the pun).

When our meals came, we swapped food. I took his bread rolls and extra water, as I was thirsty, and I think I gave him my cake.

When the plane stopped, it felt odd to just walk away from someone with whom I had clicked so easily, so I suggested we swap email addresses. Ben was heading back to the UK and had a connecting flight in Dublin. I wasn't sure if he felt the same or was just killing time. But then he started emailing me and we swapped numbers. We would talk and call regularly. Ben came up to London, and I went to visit him up North, and we became very good friends.

*

I was back in London from my semester abroad and I was now living out in Zone 3, in Wood Green, far out from central London. I was again living in a house share, but I was getting much better with this setup. I tended to choose houses with multiple nationalities and older people, as it seemed to work best. I would get the tube in to Holloway Road for my lectures. At 10:30am one Monday, I walked to Wood Green tube station and tapped my Oyster card. I liked travelling midmorning, as the trains were quiet. I was on the escalator on the way down, and there was a guy who was kind of scruffy, wearing a khaki-green jacket with longish hair and jeans. He was also going down, and there was one other lady. The tube platform was very empty. I stood with my backpack on my back waiting for the train to approach. The tube lights came in from the tunnel, and suddenly I saw the guy with the long hair fling himself forwards. His body kind of went sideways in front of the train. The train screeched and put its brakes on, but it had already hit him.

I ran up the escalator all the way home. I was in shock and couldn't find my key. I just knocked and knocked on the front door of the house where I was living, until one of my flatmates opened the door. At that, I started crying and shaking, saying "The tube … the man … tube … dead."

She hugged me and started to panic, asking, "Has there been another bombing?"

I shook my head and sobbed, trying to explain what had happened, but I couldn't articulate it. Instead, my words were frenetic. I finally calmed down and told her what had happened. I kept visualising the moment that he'd jumped, and this played over and over in my head.

I decided to make my way back to university on the bus. I had to walk past the tube station, and saw that it was closed with a sign outside saying "Man under". I'd never known what that meant, but now realised that when they say "man under", that's literally what it means: somebody has jumped and is under the train.

That morning, I took two buses to university, having missed my first lecture. For two weeks, I kept getting the bus (which took three times as long). I wouldn't get a tube because it was too traumatic. I again went to counselling at the university in London, but only once or twice, because I felt the counsellor wasn't very good. He basically said that I had to just get over it. I decided to contact the counsellor in America, with whom I had kept in touch, and he said that there was nothing I could have done to have changed what had happened. We explored why people might do it, and the difference between someone standing at the edge of the tube platform or on the top of a mountain and feeling drawn in, as opposed to someone actually deciding what they are going to do. This really helped me cope with what I had seen, and I was grateful that the American counsellor was so kind to help me again.

*

By the time I turned 21, I had been living in London for nearly three years, and I had, at this stage, collected multiple groups of friends from all walks of life. I had my birthday party in Ireland. Many of my London friends had never been there, so it was a perfect opportunity for them to visit. Gabriella, my previous flatmate, had come over and was staying in my family home.

"Hannah," she said, "you keep your pots and pans in the bedroom, no?"

I could no longer avoid explaining the real reason to her.

"Actually, you know how I said that was an Irish thing? It's just a weird Hannah thing." We had a nice little giggle about it all.

At the party, my guests consisted of friends of all ages, James, Aoife (the lady from the 99p store, who at this stage was studying to be an Educational Psychologist), Gabriella, Eva, my lovely Slovakian flatmate from Wood Green who was in her late 30s along with multiple other people. Mum said it was like the United Nations, there were so many different cultures and ages at the party.

I looked around at my party and I remember thinking it was perfect! It was exactly what I wanted. Everybody who was there was very special, but it wasn't your typical 21st; everybody wasn't 21 or a relative. It was a collection of important and special people, each having played a very significant role in my life. Some had played leading roles, and others had supporting roles, but I really valued the people in that room. I realise that I never had the typical group of 15 or 20 people all the same age, growing up and being part of a gang, but what I did have was people who honestly cared about me and accepted me for who I was and what I was – people I cherished and cared for deeply.

After my 21st, I returned to London with only few months left of my degree. I was back living in halls for the final stint of my studies, and had been volunteering with Youth at Risk, using drama techniques to facilitate workshops. After I submitted my last assignment and had finished our final-year production, I stayed in London working as a production manager for an inclusive theatre company which a previous lecturer on my degree course was now running. I loved this role, working with such creative, caring, and hardworking people. They were accepting of difference, and they also valued what I and others had to offer.

When the show I was producing finished its run, I returned to Dublin.

Chapter Four: Adulthood

Aim for the moon because, if you miss, you'll end up among the
stars.

- *W. Clement Stone*

In university, I learnt so much more than the art of acting. I developed life skills and experienced my first taste of freedom. Now I had my degree, I was ready to start fulfilling my other ambitions and I wanted to see more of the world.

My younger brother Killian attended a charity organisation which offered support and services for people with disabilities, but they didn't have staff that had Irish Sign Language (ISL), which is what he used to communicate. From a young age, while I was still in primary school, I used to help Killian with his personal care, and as an adolescent, I would often attend events and activities with him, supervising him and helping him to engage with others.

There was a residential summer camp that Killian was invited to, but they didn't have anyone with ISL, so when I was 17, I volunteered to go with him for the week. We shared a room, and I interpreted for him, helped mind him, looked after his personal care and assisted with all of the other activities in which he needed support.

I really enjoyed the experience, but the following year I was at university and needed to earn money, as I had a student bank loan. I had got myself a summer job in a department store on Henry Street, so I couldn't do the summer camp with him. But the head of relief staff and the organisers asked if I would come in for an interview. I applied, mainly so that I could do the summer camp with Killian. It was all very formal; I had to send my CV in, and in the actual interview, there was a panel of three interviewing me.

One of the questions they asked me was, "What happens if you are working with someone who is 18, and you have to help them with their personal care? How would you feel?"

"It's not about me," I said. "It doesn't matter how I feel. I'm just there to facilitate them to do what they need to do; as long as they are comfortable, its fine."

I remember that, afterwards, we were discussing this a little bit more, and they said, "That's quite a profound statement for a 19-year-old to make."

I knew what it was like to need support; it's about them helping me do something without making me feel that I am lacking. I had been very lucky that over the years I had found some wonderful people to help me, and I wanted to do the same for others.

I got the job at the disability organisation, and originally just worked there in the summer camps and mainly with my younger brother. But then I also got other children allocated to me, and was asked to do nursery cover and residential care for adults. I really enjoyed it. A lot of it was carrying out personal care, because initially it was a Care Assistant kind of role: feeding, washing, and supervising. It evolved into my getting more complex clients to work who often had marked communication challenges and I was up-trained in challenging behaviour. I found that work quite interesting. It became more social as opposed to physical care. When I started working with people with sensory processing disorder and seeing them doing unusual things like I used to do, I would think, *I know what that feels like. I know why they are doing that.* I would try to understand their triggers. I found that, because of this understanding, I was very good at interacting and working with children and adults with sensory behaviours.

I used to work two weeks of the residential summer camp. For years, I did week one and week three of the camp. For some reason, in 2007, I had finished university late and was not able to do week one and week three, so I opted to do weeks two and four. It was probably my fourth or fifth year of doing the camps. As people were arriving, I was singing to some of the kids in the conservatory, and just stopped when I saw him – another staff member, a guy wearing light blue jeans and a white T-shirt with the collar up. He had auburn hair, and his arms were crossed. His name was Colm. I made eye contact with him for a second, and had to look away immediately. I was very attracted to this guy, but I didn't know anything about him.

Over the week at the camp, you are at your worst. You really see people's personalities because you are all living in a very small space. We probably got one afternoon off during the week, and that was it. Colm was a physiotherapist who had opted to go on the summer camp in order to get time in lieu. He had apparently done the second week of this camp for the previous two years, but we hadn't met as I had always done weeks one and three. In the evenings, the staff would all sit around as a group chatting, and he was a charismatic, articulate, interesting, and caring guy. On the final night of the camp, the staff did a performance for the kids of "Dancing Queen", and dressed up. Even Colm got involved and was a good sport.

After our show, we put on a disco for the kids. I was dancing with some of the kids, and I ended up slipping and falling on my bum and hurting my leg. It was not unusual of me to fall.

I sat down beside Colm, and said, "Oh, I've just whacked my leg."

Being a physio, he offered to take a look and said, "It'll be fine. You just need some ice."

And then, out of nowhere, I said to him, "Do you fancy a cup of coffee or something sometime?"

His jaw dropped and he was like, "Uh ... absolutely!"

"Okay," I said, "let's swap numbers."

After the camp, we went on a few dates, to museums, in to town, to parks, etc. One evening, he was driving us to a castle outside Dublin. We had been seeing each other for a little while, and I asked, "What are we?"

He said, "I guess we're boyfriend and girlfriend."

I said, "No, we are not – we never agreed that; you never asked me."

At that, Colm pulled the car over into a layby and said, "Hannah, will you be my girlfriend?"

I accepted, and from there things progressed.

*

Ben, who I had met on my return flight from America, had moved to Australia. In late 2007, I went to visit him, and we went travelling all around Australia together for a few weeks. We flew to the Whitsundays. I was on a very tight budget, so we were staying in hostels and shared rooms. I was 21, and he was older, so we had very different lifestyles. I had just finished being a student and had worked for a few months, saving up so I could go travelling. We decided to do all the touristy, once-in-a-lifetime places. We wanted to do Fraser Island. It was cheaper, safer, and more fun to do in a group, so we joined a holiday group. They put 12 people together and gave them a minibus and three tents, along with the boat tickets to get to the island, and maps. Apart from Ben, everyone else was a complete stranger to me. Now, I am not very good at being in untidy places or sharing my space with other people, so the way I coped with this situation was by being "Mummy". Even though I was one of the youngest people on the trip I cooked all the dinners. In that way, I would know that everything was clean and safe. I may have lied and told them that I was really good at directions because I couldn't cope with sitting all squished in the back for very long. Three people could sit in the front: the driver, the person giving directions, and another seat which we alternated. I didn't allow my disabilities to prevent me from experiencing things that lots of other people get to experience, but I did manage to find a way to cope with these difficulties. I think it helped having Ben there as he was a relaxed and supportive friend to be around.

Colm came over to Australia too. He was studying in Perth for a month, and flew to meet me and his brother in Sydney. One evening, Colm took me to a revolving cocktail bar overlooking the Sydney skyline. I decided tonight was going to be the first night I had an alcoholic drink, and it was going to be a Pina Colada. I wore a black sparkly cocktail dress and it all seemed just perfect, only I had never had a drink before. I only had one Pina Colada, following which I felt hyper and giddy. I remember going to the toilet and then coming out feeling disorientated. I couldn't find my way back to our table and Colm. I had not been able to grasp the whole revolving restaurant bit, and the room was literally spinning, too. Later, when we got back to the apartment, I tried to sneak out that night, as I wanted to go to a party. It was like me on coffee but five times worse. Colm decided that I was not safe to be let out on my own! The next day, we had arranged to go to Sydney Zoo, but I felt so unwell like I had flu, and the ground seemed to keep moving. I decided to retire from drinking after that one and only drink!

*

In 2008 when I was 22, I entered the Rose of Tralee competition again, but this time in Dublin. It was a very different setup and scale compared to the London competition. The Dublin competition had 10 times the amount of entrants, and I remember thinking, *Wow, some of these girls were very impressive.* They had a couple of different heats, and then all the successful girls got to go to the final. I was lucky and got to the final round. After we had done the interviews and stage performance, they brought all of us ladies back on stage and announced my name as the Dublin Rose. I couldn't understand. "What, sorry, what are they saying?" I asked. All the girls on stage turned to me and a few started to hug me, and I just froze and burst into tears. I properly bawled; you would swear someone had told me that I had lost something. I was in shock because I really didn't think I was actually going to win it, having not won in a smaller competition in London a few years previously. I just cried and cried. All of the photographs of me receiving my tiara and bouquet of flowers show me with my mouth open, tears rolling down my face, and big rosy cheeks.

I did it. I was going to fulfil one of my childhood dreams and be a Rose on television in the Dome in Tralee. I was the Dublin representative, and was heading to Tralee with 32 other girls from around the world for two weeks of events, ending with the big televised event itself. The first week consisted of a road trip where we stayed in wonderful hotels, had presents on our pillows, and did shop openings and charity work. I got dozens of dresses given to me by shops and designers. As part of my prize in Dublin, I got to work with a designer to make me a dress for the live show. This was referred to as the "television dress". I went to meet the designer, and while I was waiting, I saw a white wedding dress that looked so soft and comfortable. I asked her if I could try it on; it was as comfortable as it had looked, and was elegantly beautiful. I suggested that we might select a dark green fabric and recreate the design for me. She did an amazing job on it.

There were also lots of interviews for newspapers, television, and radio. In Tralee, they have parades and autograph-signing events where the Rose is treated like a celebrity. Children would look to collect messages and signatures from each of the Roses. I was very conscious of my capacity to write these notes because of spelling and handwriting, so I asked Tralee to arrange a stamp saying, "*Best wishes, the Dublin Rose*". When I was on stage being interviewed, the presenter asked me particularly about my dyslexia and dyspraxia, and how it affects me. It was probably the first time that I really started speaking about my difficulties in public.

In the hotels, you shared a room with another Rose; I shared with an Australian Rose. In the adjoining room were two other Roses. We had an interconnecting door, so the four of us were sharing one space. One of the girls in the adjoining room was Jane, the New Zealand Rose, and she and I clicked immediately. Jane and I were a similar dress size, so we would share clothes and help each other to get ready. We would put each other's tan on in the evening, and plan outfits because we would have to change our outfits two to three times per day: we could be going from a church or a library to the horse races (daywear), and then need an evening gown for the evening event (a ball or a parade). All of the girls were so friendly, which was really strange for me, because I had never really been a part of a big group of "girly" girls like this, with everyone sharing with and supporting one another. It was like something out of a film – a dream come true.

Once I had won the Dublin Rose of Tralee competition, I ended up getting asked to do fashion shows, lots of photoshoots and charity events. I then joined a modelling agency around that time and started to do a few more shoots. Some of them were just portfolio shoots, or "tiffs", as they call them.

I enjoyed it and got to meet some really creative people. I also got a few paid gigs for campaigns, and some more press call-type shoots and editorials.

The most exciting gig, I suppose, was the one that I was most anonymous in. This was when I was told to turn up for a casting and to make sure that my hands were nice. I am lucky, as I have quite long nails, but I don't paint them or get them manicured. When I turned up, I found out it was hand casting for the Sony Record label. I had to make different shapes with my hands.

I got a phone call the next day telling me that I had been booked for a job, and I was going to be on the album cover for a band called The Script. I had to make sure that I didn't break a nail or damage my hands in the next 24 hours before the shoot.

I cancelled the swimming that I was going to go to in case the chlorine weakened my nails. And knowing me and my ability to be accident prone, I had to be very careful.

During the photo shoot, there were three or four different hands being photographed. There was mine, a child's hand, an elderly person's hand, and a male hand. Me and the male hand were holding hands and doing different poses.

When the album came out, it was my hand on the front of the single and on the album, as well as the posters to advertise the new album. There was also a TV advertisement, which was a series of snaps of my hand and the male model's hand making images.

The Script was huge and my hand was everywhere. I think it's quite poignant that the hands that struggled with writing, tying shoe laces and holding cutlery were now, even with my scar, being shown everywhere. It was probably the biggest modelling job that I was booked for.

*

After I briefly talked about having dyslexia and dyspraxia on the Rose of Tralee, a lot of people had written in to the Rose of Tralee office to make contact with me. On the second night of the television broadcast, an email came for me. I remember asking one of the Roses to read it to me while we were getting our makeup done. The two of us and the makeup artist were all in tears as we read the email. A mother had written to me about her child and how grateful they were that I had spoken about dyslexia and dyspraxia so elegantly on television, and that she reckoned I had no idea what an impact that had made on her daughter and other people.

I received a huge amount of other emails, calls, and text messages, via multiple channels, from people wanting to contact me. Mainly, I was contacted by parents and disability organisations. One man contacted me who was very different to the rest; he was a lecturer at MIT, originally from India, and living in Kerry at the time. He invited me to come and do a talk in Kerry. I wasn't quite sure what the subject matter of the talk should be.

"Just come down and tell me a bit about your life," he said. "Put some slides together. We have some other speakers."

There was one other speaker besides myself: Sir Clive Granger, who was a winner of the Nobel Prize in Economic Sciences.

I agreed to do the talk because I had never met a Nobel Prize winner, never mind sharing a speaking platform with one, and was honoured to be invited back down to Tralee. They said they would cover my expenses, and would book my flights and hotel, and it would take two days in total. I still wasn't quite sure what a presentation should look like; if it had written words, I would struggle to read it, even if the words were my own. As I learn best visually, I decided to scan a load of photographs of me from different stages in my life and put them in a PowerPoint presentation to use as cues to guide my train of thought.

My first audience was 1,000 secondary-school students. Sir Clive went first, and then I went second. I just started telling my story and talking about things that I thought were interesting. At the end, the whole school stood up and gave me a standing ovation, and some of the students had tears in their eyes. I could tell they had been really listening, as they had stopped fidgeting, which they had been doing earlier in the seminar, when I spoke. I got a big bunch of flowers and was thanked profusely.

We then went to the Institute of Technology and presented in front of the faculty, and again, I just put up my photographs and spoke in my own words, telling my own stories. I didn't quite know what people were looking for me to do or say, and again, it was received really well – so much so that when I went back to Dublin, I was phoned a few weeks later and asked if I would be interested in coming back and doing a talk for some people studying to be entrepreneurs, at another school, and a couple of other university groups. Of course I agreed, because I really enjoyed the process of standing up and discussing things, and answering questions. It was also therapeutic for me, because some of my experiences as a child were very unique to me, like the "I Hate Hannah Club" and other things. Now I was finally able to understand, articulate my experiences, and speak up for that child. So if I could help other children in that situation just by sharing my story, wasn't that worth doing? This MIT academic and his family are still important friends of mine.

After doing those talks, I was approached by the Dyspraxia Association, a few other charities in Dublin, and occupational therapists, and asked to talk specifically to parents of children with dyslexia and dyspraxia. Every time I would give my talk, I would change it slightly, depending on my audience. As it was not scripted, and was arranged around photographs, different stories would come out each time. Depending on what the people in the audience would ask me, I would share more information, addressing their specific questions. I was asked to give talks to Special Needs Assistants, teachers, and others. Many newspapers seemed to be interested in what I was doing and were picking up the talks in their articles. I was asked to be the Keynote Speaker at the Dyspraxia Conference. I somehow ended up being on The Late Late Show, which is one of Ireland's largest and longest-running chat shows and the most viewed show in Ireland, speaking very publicly about my difficulties.

From there, I did a lot more television, radio, newspapers, and magazine reports on various aspects of my life. It all really stemmed from being open about my difficulties, but what people found more interesting was how I managed to do what I do and get where I am despite having those needs or extra difficulties.

Adulthood

Photo taken by Christophe Majani d'Inguimbert

Photo taken by Eoghan Brennan

Photo taken by Barry McCall

My siblings (photo by Arthur Carron)

My Mum

My Husband Colm

My wonderful children

Chapter Five: A Crossroads

What's for you won't pass you by.

- *Anon.*

I loved acting. I always had a definite idea that I was going to be an actress. It was what motivated me to stay in school and later in university. But during this part of my adult life, I also realised that I was passionate about wanting to help people with additional challenges achieve their goals. I am a firm believer in the adage, *What's for you won't pass you by*, but I also knew that I needed to be proactive in making things happen.

I had an interview for a drama teacher position at a further education college, and following my interview, I was offered the position. It was only on a part-time basis, which suited me due to other commitments I had. Initially, I started teaching 14 adult students who all had learning disabilities. From the outset, my main focus was how to make the curriculum accessible to all of my students. My priority was to differentiate the curriculum in a way that would make sure that all of my students' learning needs were being met, and ensure that they could achieve their best.

Interestingly, my students were very creative individuals themselves, and displayed a mix of ability and different skill sets. I often found that pairing certain students together would lead to a wonderful piece of work, facilitating both students to excel. In the beginning of the drama sessions, we often did a "Check In", where everybody would hold a beanbag, say how they were, talk a little bit about themselves, and pass the beanbag on. This was really the most valuable aspect of the drama sessions for the students, because they were actually given a voice and were able to say how they felt. Others would respond, "Yeah, I feel that way too!" or, "That's a horrible sensation!", and acknowledge one another's feelings. One thing that would come out in a lot of the drama pieces we were doing was a sense of powerlessness, a sense of a lack of ability to control their lives and have their say. In the class, there were people who were 21 years old, and others who were 45 years old. There was an obvious generation gap which was reflected in a changing societal attitude towards disability, and the younger students tended to be a lot more independent than the older students.

I directed and devised performances with the students, including *Romeo and Juliet* and some contemporary pieces. The performances allowed the students to put themselves out there and be seen. The students loved coming to the classes and made enormous progress.

I was asked if I would consider running the Self Advocacy further education programme, too. I was delighted to, as I felt that this course was important for these adults. I needed to teach this topic in a non-patronising way, and I knew I could do this. My aim was to give a forum for people with disabilities to actually have their voices heard and for them to become comfortable using their voices in a respectful environment. I also wanted to facilitate finding a voice for those who had difficulty with language.

As part of the programme, I decided to invite a speaker to talk to everybody about human rights, and the students' rights, specifically. The person who came was a wheelchair user who had no function in his arms. Ironically, some of my students turned around and said, "Oh, that poor man! He is very disabled! He can't do anything!"

I said, "Why do you think that?"

"Because look at him," they said. "He is in a wheelchair."

It was interesting to see that some of my students, who had been discriminated against themselves had the notion that a person in a wheelchair must be helpless, sad, and powerless. Their response surprised me.

This speaker was a very inspiring man: the movie *Inside I'm Dancing* is actually based on his experience and how his disability had a huge impact on his life.

On another occasion in one of the classes, a student spoke about having Down syndrome.

Another girl who had Down syndrome got upset and said, "Don't say that word! It's a horrible word! You're not allowed say Down syndrome – it's a bad word!"

Yet another student turned around and said, "Well, *I* have Down syndrome, too."

I tried to facilitate an honest, open discussion, but was also mindful of the girl's emotional response to that word. I was equally aware of the need to support the confidence and sense of self of the young man who was proud of having Down syndrome. It was clear that some of the group were oblivious to what Down syndrome was. Perhaps this stemmed from the notion that their parents wanted to "protect" or "shelter" them, but I've always found that notion difficult to understand. The self-advocacy sessions were a space to explore and be respectful of self and others, and I learnt so much from working with these students.

*

At the same time as I was teaching, I was also acting, and was cast as the lead girl in a final-year student short for a film school in Dublin. In the final scene, my character breaks into freestyle dancing. I still struggled with rhythm, but the director told me to just dance in the safety of my room like no one was watching. That's when I realised I have rhythm, but it is my own kind of rhythm. I broke into my freestyle dancing, which was recorded for one of the last scenes in the film. It was shown in the cinema, and the next day there was an article that said that the highlight of the whole movie was the moment when I broke into dancing:

that there was a freedom or rawness in how I moved, and such expression in that scene. How ironic, as I had always been seen as "the girl with no rhythm who can't dance".

Following that, I seemed to land a lot of parts which had very little vocal or speaking aspects, but had quite a significant visual component. I was in a short film in which I had the lead, but I think I said about two sentences throughout the film. Perhaps this was because when I auditioned I didn't have to read a full script, so it made it easier for me to actually act as opposed to being caught up in trying to get the script beforehand and learn it off by heart. To try to read or be fed lines doesn't really work, because I would be trying to retain a line that I had just heard for the first time. I would be stressed that I wouldn't be able to read the script, or they may have given me another script or a different character, which would throw me.

I was then contacted by a film director who was casting for a paid feature film. He had seen photos of me and decided that I had the right look for a part. When I met him, I found out the role that he was looking for me to play was the lead. I was very nervous and brutally honest, and said, "Don't you think I am a bit young for the part?" I didn't have the self-belief needed to pull off a full lead. He was so nice and we chatted more about the film's premise. After our meeting, he contacted me to say that he had decided that he was going to go with someone else for the lead part, but that he wanted to offer me a different role in the film. He thought that I could play the role of a palliative care nurse. I was delighted with my first paid acting gig, which comprised of three days filming. I met the woman who was cast as the lead, and was disappointed when I realised she was not that much older than me but was a lot more confident.

After that, I was cast in two or three music videos, again always playing the lead, which involved strong expression and lots of physical movement, but not a lot of speaking. Over the years, I have played a variety of characters, from a heroin addict to a palliative care nurse. I was sent to auditions by my agent, usually for commercials or film projects, but I never did well in them because I didn't quite know how to gauge the atmosphere and what interaction I was to have with the casting director. I had a lot of anxiety around the performance and the script, and the waiting and anticipation. I just didn't do well in that environment. When it came to actually performing, being creative, and understanding a character, I excelled. The audition was the barrier.

The other difficulty for me with the acting was that it was up and down: one week you could be doing two or three projects with others lined up, and then you could have months and months with nothing. That was very difficult for me, in particular not having any sense of control over it, which I suppose is similar for a lot of people. I still hadn't managed to sort out my anxiety about the reading component that is often involved with auditioning. I know that there are many world-famous actors with dyslexia, but I didn't ever fully master the script reading and auditioning process.

*

In 2008, my brother Stuart was diagnosed with a complex and rare disorder, and the hospital suggested looking at all of our family members to see if there were any matches to make a stem cell donation (similar to a bone marrow donation). I, of course, went. I was really anxious the night before, crying, afraid of having to get my blood taken so they could see if I was a match. Of everybody who was tested, I was the only match.

The donation involved my going to Kings College Hospital in London. The first time I went over, they did blood tests and explained the process to me. The stem cell donation would involve multiple needles and injections of various sizes. On hearing this, I felt very anxious. But equally, the desire to do it far exceeded my fear of the process and any discomfort involved. Initially, they found out that I was low in iron, so I needed to take some tonics before I could donate. On the morning of my first donation, they had difficulties accessing a vein and getting a line in my arm, and that was quite stressful. The failed attempts caused some bruising. I cried my eyes out, saying, "I want to go home!" Finally, a different nurse manged to get the needles in. I had a large needle placed in both arms, one to take blood out of my body, which was then spun through a machine, the stem cells separated, and the blood was sent back to the other arm through the other needle.

Before they collected the second donation, I went to the hospital for five consecutive days, to receive injections that stimulated the growth of stem cells in my body. This made my bones feel quite swollen, my skull in particular, and my joints felt really achy, and I had a throbbing headache. Six days after my first donation, I went back and donated stem cells over two more days. Again, a really large needle went into each arm. I was a bit more familiar with the process by this time, and not as anxious. I sat watching daytime TV from the bed. Colm had come over and was waiting with me. I was suddenly bursting to go to the toilet, but because you are strapped up to a machine, you can't leave once you have started the process, nor can you bend your arms or do any kind of functional movement with your hands. And, because it's a "clean" medical environment, you are not allowed to have a proper commode or anything like that for hygiene reasons. I was given a cardboard potty which needed to be placed on a chair for me to hover over. I needed help to get off the bed and lower my leggings and underwear. I hovered over the potty. I had just about finished peeing when my calcium levels dropped and I fainted while I was strapped up to two machines and was hovering over cardboard potty filled with urine.

I woke up to see Colm and a few nurses around me, and I was soaking wet. They were trying to keep my lines away from the spilled urine and get me back onto the bed. I kept apologising and was so upset with myself. I felt dirty and embarrassed. Even though Colm had no issue with helping me get changed, nor did the nurses (as it was part of their job), I still did not like the feeling of being helpless. This was despite the fact that, by this stage, I had probably changed a hundred people and helped them with their personal care, and I had no issue with it. But being on the other end of it was not pleasant. In addition, my mood was probably quite low, and I was quite fatigued, having just done a series of donations.

The stem cells were frozen and held for when Stuart might need them. I felt huge relief. I had been worried that I would not be able to see the process through. I was glad it was over, and I was so relieved that the stem cells were banked and ready.

It took me a few weeks to recover but it was definitely worth it. Stuart got me the biggest, tackiest card, and thanked me for being his *Blood Brother.*

*

Colm and I had been going out for a few years, and he was taking me away on a weekend surprise, so I was to pack a bag. We went to the Powerscourt House and Gardens. Probably three or four years previous to that, Colm and I had gone to the Powerscourt Gardens, maybe four or five dates into our relationship, and being the kid that I am, I asked Colm to roll down the hill with me.

Colm was very uptight, especially in comparison to the free spirit that I was, but he agreed to roll down the hill, telling me he hadn't done it in years.

On this, our second visit to the Powerscourt Gardens, we first came to the beautiful tower in the Japanese Garden and climbed it. It was all very romantic. Then it started to rain and the grass was all damp, but Colm said, "Let's roll down the hill?" I agreed to this, as long as I could wear his rain jacket, which came down to my knees, so I wouldn't get too wet.

We were rolling down the hill, holding hands, and I kind of head-butted Colm and got wet. I jumped up and said, "No, this is silly."

He said, "No, put your hand in the pocket, please," as I was now wearing his coat.

I put my hand in and picked out a box. I just handed it back to him and said, "No."

We didn't talk about it, and continued walking around the park, with me complaining that my jeans were damp and muddy.

147

Later on, we were sitting on a bench looking up at the big house. Colm got down on one knee and I started shaking my head again. Colm said, "Look, Hannah. I love you to bits. I'm not going to ask you a third time. Will you marry me?"

I was still kind of shaking my head. Then he opened the box, and I said, "Yes, okay," and he put the ring on my finger. Initially, I was overwhelmed. I needed grounding. I sat on Colm's lap and tucked my knees under my chin, while he wrapped his arms tightly around me, and I knew I had made the right choice.

After this, we went to the Ritz for afternoon tea, which was nice, but they brought the scones out first and then the tea, so it was all cold and that made me quite disappointed. The portions were small as well, and we hadn't really eaten much apart from a little breakfast. We then went upstairs. Colm said we were just going up to drop a bag off or something, when actually he had arranged a suite. There was a big bunch of beautiful sunflowers, which are my favourite. It was a massive room with a separate sitting room and two bathrooms. Colm went to the toilet and couldn't find me when he came back; I was sitting in a walk-in wardrobe crying my eyes out.

"What's wrong?" he asked. "Do you not want to marry me?"

"No," I said, "it's just not how I imagined it. I feel a bit overwhelmed."

"Why did you pick the smallest, darkest place?" he said. "There are other places you could have sat crying." We both laughed.

I had imagined a different proposal, with a picnic basket and blanket beside a weeping willow tree, a lake, me in a white dress, sunset and sunflowers. Colm's proposal was lovely, but it was somewhat at odds with my childhood fantasy and I needed to process it. I was experiencing visual and auditory overstimulation in the hotel environment. I was hungry, tired, and overwhelmed, and I'd retreated into a dark, confined space to calm.

We decided that we would go to the (familiar) Avoca cafe, where we got hot chocolate and a Rice Crispy cake to tide us over. Colm had booked Gordon Ramsey's restaurant for dinner that evening. He had arranged a special dessert and the staff made a huge fuss. When we returned to the suite, there were rose petals scattered and candles lit. It was perfect.

I'd always had it in my head that I was going to get married in Italy, and luckily Colm didn't object. In fact, he really liked the idea of getting married there. We found a beautiful venue in the middle of nowhere, very rustic and authentic. The venue was relaxed and was happy to accommodate whatever we wanted. I wanted a small wedding, with only people who actually wanted to be there. In the end, we had 65 people. We had a very young wedding.

It was a three-day event. The first day was a barbecue, the second day the wedding, and the third day was another barbecue.

It was magical, and it was simple. Even on the day of our wedding, I went swimming in the pool with all of my friends.

At the dinner table, when people were giving speeches, I decided to stand up and give a speech. Not pre-planned or anything, but I decided, why not, it's my wedding, too, and I was only addressing friends, so it didn't really matter.

149

For the third and last day, we had organised a sports day with tug of war, wheelbarrow races, egg-and-spoon races, and sack races. It was great fun. That evening, after dinner, we had arranged for a room with a piano, as lots of our friends are musicians and performers, or have hidden talents. Everybody did a sing-song dancing session, which went on for six hours. There is even footage of everybody singing "Bohemian Rhapsody", which is quite funny. People who wouldn't usually get involved all joined in.

I was happy with my wedding because my expectations were met, but also because it wasn't trying to be anything it wasn't. It was just rustic and authentic, and the people I liked were there doing nice things. I was being true to myself. I guess it took a long few years before I was able to be that, to find someone I can be myself with, and to have a selection of friends who are very special with whom I can be myself, value and feel valued in return.

*

Having worked for years running social skills workshops and advocating for people with disabilities, I decided to retrain as an occupational therapist (OT). I submitted a very strong application detailing my experience to date, and why I wanted to be an OT. I also submitted some essays that were required as part of the application process. I got called to interview for three universities.

I emailed the first university which offered an interview to say that I had dyslexia and I would require some assistance with the interview process, as there were several written components to the interview. I was told that this would not be a problem, and that there would be a student available to assist me on the day. I declared myself when I arrived and there were students available to tell us where to go.

During the written exam, I went up and explained who I was, that I had dyslexia, and that I would require some writing assistance. They said that was fine and that I could have someone to assist me. Then they said we needed to go and find a room. So we had to search the whole university to find a spare classroom to do the exam. The rest of the group of interviewees had all started the written exam, whereas I had to traipse around and find a classroom.

The first classroom we went into was empty, so we sat down. It was a timed piece, and the student started to read, but he was struggling.

I said, "Are you all right?"

He said, "Oh, I've got dyslexia, you see."

I thought this was absolutely brilliant. I'd gotten somebody who had the same difficulties as me to assist me in an area in which I have difficulties. Granted, his dyslexia wasn't as profound as mine, but he was struggling with reading and writing certain words: when I was giving my responses, he was saying, "Well, how do you spell that?" and I had to say, "I'm really sorry, but I don't know."

In the middle of my exam, some lecturers came in and said that they had booked the room, and we had to leave. So we had to get up and go to a different classroom.

Following this, there was the individual interview as well as a group interview. The group interview again had reading and writing components, and I asked some of the other interviewees to assist me with that aspect. Finally, in the actual individual interview, the main focus of their questioning was around my dyslexia, and how I would be able to cope and manage doing a Master's degree as I have additional needs.

I came home and recorded my experience because I found it to be completely wrong. It was a little like inviting someone in a wheelchair to attend an interview, and then asking them to either crawl up the stairs or offering to carry them up: it is not actually making something accessible. It was demoralising and a very embarrassing experience for me.

Had I been offered a place at that university, I would have been reluctant to accept, given my experience and my perception of their approach to inclusion. The irony was that these were occupational therapists, and not just any occupational therapists, but occupational therapists who were educating future occupational therapists!

Another university seemed a little more receptive to my difficulties. With a bit of forward planning, they emailed me the day before I was due to do the interview with the text piece so that I could listen to it prior to attending. We had agreed that I would do the reflection piece on a dictaphone, and then it would be typed up afterwards and emailed to them.

At the actual interview, we did a group problem-based learning activity, but instead of using the text that they had sent me, they decided to change it at the last minute, and printed off a quote, asking us to discuss it. This threw me, for obvious reasons. They read the new statement out only once, and everyone else studied and reread the text multiple times. There was not a huge amount of detail in it, so it was more reflective, but I still found this quite stressful.

Following the interview, I did my reflection and sent it to them, and I did query the fact that I had been expecting something different.

They said, "We wanted to throw you to see how you coped with change. We were thinking afterwards that, as the course is delivered using a problem-based learning approach, new information is often presented during the session."

I felt at a disadvantage, having been put in a situation which I thought would be accessible and suddenly it wasn't. I was also treated differently after the interview because we were meant to find out the very next week if we had been successful or unsuccessful. I got a holding letter saying that they hadn't decided yet. Other people with whom I had gone to the interview, who had been in Ireland, had either been told yes or no. When I was asked, I had to say, "Well, I don't know yet."

Finally, I got a letter saying that they had decided that I wasn't going to be offered a place, which really disappointed me because the whole process was *almost* accessible and then at the end I was treated differently.

My third interview was for my first-choice university, because it meant that I could be in the same city as Colm, who was also doing a Master's degree. The Student Disability Services were not able to provide a scribe or reader for the interview because there was no funding, as I was not a registered student. The faculty as a whole, however, agreed to give me a member of staff who volunteered to do the reading and writing aspect of my interview so that I could engage fully. Again, there were multiple layers to the interview process, not just the written component.

I was delighted leaving that interview. Regardless of whether I got a place, I felt that I had been given an opportunity, that I was respected and treated like an equal, and had been able to show what I knew and my potential. If I wasn't accepted, it would be based purely on my performance and my ability, rather than what they decided I was worth.

Sometime after the interview, I phoned the university because I was wondering whether I needed to start applying for jobs in London or whether I was going to do the MSc course in Occupational Therapy. When I was told, "Yes – we are offering you a place", I burst into tears. I was going to be an occupational therapist!

*

I wanted to learn to drive, but I had a very long lead-in to the process. I first needed a learner permit, and to do that, I needed to pass the driver theory test. This test involved sitting at a computer and answering multiple choice questions. The screens were touch sensitive, and there was a possibility of getting a "computer voice" to read the questions and possible answers to you. My first attempt at the theory test involved my trying to get the computer to read. It was not explained to me how to do it, so I was actually selecting the answers rather than hitting on the correct part to make it read. I remember leaving the theory test, having failed, and feeling devastated. Very few people fail, because it is generally considered very easy. But the next time I did my theory test, I was familiar with the technology and got full marks.

Next came actually learning to drive. I decided that, since I was petrified of the process, I was going to pay for it and do proper lessons in a car with someone else who had another set of pedals just in case. I was working in a residential care setting, and the father of one of the clients was a driving instructor. I decided that he was going to be the one to teach me how to drive; he was really patient, had a nice jovial energy, and took it really slow. I must have done 10 or more lessons with him, and this was before you were even required to take driving lessons. During one lesson, I was driving us around a little housing estate. I was only in second gear and just about comfortable with it. The driving instructor was giving me directions, which was essentially doing mini loops. Then he said, "Okay now, the next time we go around, I want you to take the left," which went onto a semi main road. Initially, I said no, and he said, "Hannah, take the next left."

At that, I swore and said, "I won't; I can't – I'll kill us if I do!" I had driven past the left turn by now, and he was so calm. As I came to the turn again, he instructed me the same as before: to take the next left. I trusted him and felt a little more confident. I was happy to do some of the things that felt a bit scary, like going out into the main road while being responsible for the car.

I also then went on Colm's insurance and tried to drive him and his friends around after nights out as I'm a non-drinker, but it was a different kind of car and it didn't feel right.

On the date of the driving test, I felt really confident and was ready for it, and had booked my instructor's car. As soon as we pulled up, I remember my driving instructor murmuring, "Oh …" because he could see whom I was allocated. I did well on that exam, but failed on a few little things, which I felt, was a bit unfair. I decided to repeat the test because I was going to London and wouldn't have access to a car. I sat the retest within a week. The second time I did the test, I was not focused; I was thinking about my previous test, and I failed. I left for London without my licence, but I had made progress.

*

From a very early age, I tried multiple types of technology and software to help me with my difficulties. One Christmas, I got a spellchecker in my stocking, which really upset me; it was an old-school type of thing, almost like a calculator. I also got books and videotapes with titles like, *I Can Read! I Can Read!* in which you would blast off to space and have to spell words.

In secondary school, I was given computer software which was made especially for people who were visually impaired. You would have to scan documents using a particular kind of scanner and it would read certain components of it, but really slowly and in a Stephen Hawking-type voice. I also tried several versions of both a dictation software and a reading tool.

None of these really worked for me. Their level of sophistication wasn't great; the voice was not natural, and it often shut down midway through a task, as it took up a lot of memory on the computer and conflicted with other programmes.

When I started my Master's in Occupational Therapy, I was loaned an iPad by the university. I came across a brilliant text to speech iPad app which cost me £1.49. It converted PDF files to mp3s, to which you could listen. I often contacted publishers of the books that I had purchased and requested that they gave me a copy of the book in a PDF format. I then used this software to enable me to access the book in mini chunks. This wouldn't have worked before – I would never have listened to a chapter of a book using the other software options. They were more something that I would use if I really needed to find out bits of information. I would use these previous options to listen to information in order to get by, whereas the text to speech app was more enjoyable and didn't make me as frustrated. I could therefore focus on actually taking in the information. Sometimes things would go wrong: for example, it would say "the first of March" if "1.3" was written.

One of our first sessions on the Occupational Therapy course was by a representative from the College of Occupational Therapists, who was doing a one-hour lecture on the benefits of being a member of the College and their role. As she was a guest lecturer, she was unfamiliar with the building, the technology, and the setup.

The lecture hall was on the sixth floor, and during her talk, there was a high-pitched "BZZZZ", quite an intense noise, as well as the fan noise of the computer. But the "BZZZZ" was so distracting that when I was trying to block out the fan noise and zone into what the lecturer was saying, it gave me a headache.

As I was finding it very difficult to actually follow what she was presenting, I put my hand up and asked if she could do anything about the noise, but she couldn't as she was unfamiliar with the setup and she just continued.

I couldn't take it anymore: I had to sit still, take in information, while trying to block out the buzzing noise. I was actually starting to feel quite sick, and I had to get up and leave the session.

I went downstairs to the receptionist and explained the problem, and asked if they would be able to send anyone up. They said that they would, but it would be another 20 minutes. I went back up and sat outside the room, waiting until someone came and resolved the problem. I was very stressed because I was missing out on her presentation, but decided that it was better that I didn't get wound up, and I wasn't actually taking in any of the information anyway because of the noise; I was better off staying relaxed so that I could go to the other lectures that followed. But at the same time, I was disappointed that I was not able to participate fully in the curriculum. (I did become a member of the College of Occupational Therapists regardless of this experience, and have found them to be very helpful).

My friend Jane (the New Zealand Rose) moved over to London while I was studying for my Master's. Jane is such a supportive friend; before she had moved over to London, she was away travelling. I would send her copies of articles that I would like read, and she would record them on her computer, and email them over to me so I could have access to them. Jane would even leave me secret messages when she was reading them; she would say things like, "Hi Hannah!" … "Oh yes, I'm not sure I said this word right!", or little comments like, "That was a really interesting article", which always helped me keep alert. It was lovely having personalised readings done, especially when articles were photocopies so the software couldn't read it. I had other friends who read articles for me, too, but Jane did the most and I never felt bad or "less than" for asking her.

*

As part of training to be an occupational therapist, you go on placements. It could be eight weeks of shadowing in a specific setting, taking on occupational therapy roles, and taking notes.

You are graded in the setting, and it is the practical element of the Occupational Therapy course.

Before my first placement, educators were apprehensive about taking me because of my additional needs. At that stage, my reasonable adjustments were that I would use a computer which had a dictation software and reading software on it. Because most of the information is private in a hospital, I couldn't transfer client information onto my laptop, so I couldn't actually read any of the patients' notes using this piece of equipment. In my first placement, there was another employee who had dyslexia and who had this software on her computer, so when she wasn't in, I could use her computer to access some of the clients' notes. But it was very rare that she wasn't in.

The next issue was that I had to record my notes. I could dictate using the software on my laptop but without using the client's name e.g. saying "Client X. I would then transfer them to a USB stick and finally transfer them to the actual hospital computer. I would then delete the notes from the stick, put in the client's proper name on the real record, and file it on the system. Using this software meant that I needed to be in a quiet room, so I would need to find a room where I could dictate the notes.

For anyone who hasn't used this type of software before, it sounds wonderful: you speak, and it types. But it doesn't work that way. It doesn't transcribe accurately; it misses words, and it doesn't differentiate between homophones. I was pulled aside by my educator, who was concerned that my notes weren't good enough; she needed to read over them all the time, which she wouldn't have to do for a typical student. It wasn't the content of the notes that was the problem; it was the spelling and grammar.

There would be extra words in there, or I would say something like "tin" (as in baking tin) and it would put in "thin" (as in skinny). There were also cases of *there* and *their*, and *which* and *witch*. On top of all that, there would be one or two words that it just couldn't spell and wouldn't pick up.

It was quite frustrating because I was completing an extra two or three hours per week just to keep on top of my notes, and even then they still weren't good enough. I felt as if English was my second language, and that was how it was coming across with the types of words that I had to use – using simpler words to describe things, and then playing it back to listen and pick the problems out. It wasn't an ideal situation. The computer would also often freeze and shut down when I was in the middle of my work because the software takes up a lot of RAM.

The midway point of the placement was the most stressful. At the midway review my educator fed back that I was getting good marks in all areas, but that she was concerned as I was on the cusp of failing on the section relating to the recording of client notes. When I asked why, I was told it was due my spelling and grammar issues. When I'd get knocks or rejection like this, I'd take it very personally; I would have such a visceral response, a trigger trauma. I would be right back as a vulnerable eight-year-old girl in The Teacher's class. In these situations I have to use logic and tell myself that I am now able to stand up for myself. I am able to use my voice and protect myself. I pointed out to her that the grading system that refers to recording of notes related to the recorded content and associated decision-making, i.e. "Is the student able to analyse and record key information accurately". But that was not what she was grading me on; what she was grading me on was the accuracy of my spelling and grammar, or lack thereof!

She highlighted that her role as an educator was not to change and spell-check student notes as it was too time consuming. She also voiced her concerns regarding my ability to manage once qualified.

I got quite upset and took this personally. I said, "I don't agree with you about the grade you have given me, but I accept it." Again, someone was telling me I was not good enough based on my reading and writing ability. I was also very frustrated because from the beginning of university, I had told them that the available software didn't work for me. I had tried using it since I was 15, and it didn't work then. I understood that technology could change and improve which was why I agreed to try it again. The reality, however, was that despite the sophistication of this dictation software, it was not at the standard that it needed to be, and certainly was not for somebody who had difficulties with reading and writing. I could not identify when things went wrong particularly when it came to spelling, homophones, etc. I did not have that skill set. In order to train this software you needed to read a sample of text so that it became familiar with the way that you pronounced the words. I wasn't able to do this either.

I was concerned about the risk to my final grades. My educator arranged a meeting with a lecturer at the university where we discussed my concerns. I was quite impressed with the placement educator, because she did actually support me. She said that obviously the university's reasonable adjustments were not meeting my needs, and agreed that current software was not an adequate solution. As I had identified, I would need other support for future placements. This had been my first placement, so we hadn't necessarily anticipated all of the difficulties.

Finally, as a compromise, it was decided that the mark for the spelling of notes would be given separately to the mark for their content.

In the same placement, we used to do ward rounds, which were a series of meetings lasting several hours on Mondays. We would sit with other professionals including doctors, dieticians, physiotherapists and others, discussing the patients. I found this really difficult because the meeting rooms had no tables and chairs with no arms, and we would just have to sit there listening. For the first few weeks, I was not even involved in the discussions; I was just sitting and observing. I would find it really difficult to sit still, and I would move around a lot.

I was pulled aside and told, "You are very distracting. You are coming across as being disinterested and rude because you are moving around."

This made me feel upset because I was doing my utmost to try to stay alert, stay on a seat, and take in as much information as possible. My educator told me that attendees often brought a pen and paper to write down notes in the meeting, as it helps them to stay engaged and it looked more professional. She suggested that I do the same. This wasn't really an option for me. I was less likely to take in information if I had to concentrate on sitting really still or had to try to write. This was a bit of a paradox, because I was there to learn and try to understand as much as possible.

Some of the solutions that I came up with were to roll a cardigan up and place it under my bum. I would also put a chair in the room that had armrests on it. In addition, I started baking every Sunday night. On the Monday, I would bring in baked goods so that, in the middle of this meeting, I would produce flapjacks or lemon cakes. Everyone would naturally stand up and move around a little bit, take a cake, and have a cup of tea, and then we would sit back down again. This gave me a way of moving which was more "appropriate" and let me tolerate the ward rounds better. At lunch time, I also made sure that when I had the time, I would go for a brisk walk so that I would get rid of some of my "ants", and would do tippy-toe walking or go to the toilet. As part of the ward round, sometimes you would go and get a client, so I volunteered to be the person who went out and fetched the client from their room and walked them down to the meeting, just so I had opportunities to move. This is so important for me, because I do have low tone and it is very difficult for me to stay in a fixed position. I get achy joints because I have to lock and prop myself in order to stay in a seated position. My brain also needs movement to process information and engage. It is just who I am and what I am. Even in bed, I roll around when I am asleep, and when I watch a film, I cannot pick one that will last for more than about two hours because I know that that's my limit. When I take long flights, I get quite antsy and constantly have to move. I am sure that it is distracting for other people, but it's not me being rude or nasty: it's just what I need to do. It is how the engine in my body and head works.

In the end, my educator suggested that she would invite the university liaison person back for my final review and placement results. I said, "No, please don't, because I would like to be treated like everyone else, and I will accept the marks that you have given me, even if I don't feel that they are reflective of the work or the hours I have put in."

She respected that and agreed.

Later, I reported back to the university the problems that had arisen, and potential solutions to address some of these difficulties for me in my next placement.

The lead up to my second practice placement was very stressful because nobody felt that they could take me on again. All of the other students found out where they were going around the same time, but because I was still waiting, I was very anxious. Finally, the placement coordinator told me that they had a potential placement for me, and I was to go and meet the educator to talk about the reasonable adjustments.

The university staff member suggested that they could come with me. I said that I would like to go on my own; I had learned from my previous placement that when you have big alarm bells saying "I'm different", sometimes people look more closely at you because of it.

So I went on my own, and there were no issues. It was completely different and a much more positive experience. I was also a bit more familiar with Occupational Therapy by this time, what placements entail, and the potential difficulties.

I was again told that the use of software was problematic because of data protection and the software not being installed on the computers. There were some Occupational Therapy Assistants, who could help, and one in particular who was very good at spelling and who would have a look over my work with me. My educator would also regularly look over my work and check it.

I got on very well in this placement. The feedback at the end stated that I was aware of my difficulties, and that the support that I had in place wasn't quite meeting my needs. I was again putting in a lot of extra hours, and it also required my educator to spend time spell-checking my work rather than just assessing its content.

By the time I came to my third placement, I had been back in touch with the university to say that the situation was demoralising, as I had to use reasonable accommodation that were not working. Using software on placements wasn't working, caused more stress and that we should move to using a scribe and reader. I initially received an email from them saying that they had to look into whether using a scribe and reader would be acceptable to the Health and Care Professions Council (HCPC), and that they needed to investigate whether I would be in breach of the HCPC standards and professional codes.

I then studied every code of HCPC standards, and nowhere did it say that you are not allowed to use a scribe or reader for notes. It did say that you need to be efficient at doing your job and have the right skill sets. It was therefore seen as a reasonable adjustment that I had a reader and scribe to assist me. In fact, it was felt that it was probably more equitable, because a reader and a scribe is not a trained occupational therapist. One could argue that having an occupational therapist looking over my notes would change the meaning of the work. The university agreed to my suggestion.

My third placement was the first placement in which I had a scribe and a reader, and it was wonderful. It was the first placement where I could do assessments completely independently, write up notes, and be very efficient with my time. Having my support worker coming in three times a week meant that I was able to have all my client notes up to date and accurately recorded, with all the "i"s dotted and "t"s crossed. There were also a lot of handwritten notes in my third placement, so there was no way that I could have survived using software.

Again, it took a bit of time to get organised, trying to find rooms where I could go with my support worker. My support worker had no medical background and no real idea what Occupational Therapy was. She was very interested and would often ask me what certain terminology meant, and if she didn't know how to spell a word, she would look it up in a medical dictionary.

In my final placement, I was very lucky; this one was actually in Ireland in Paediatrics, and we were able to find a support worker who could come in and do some hours during the week. Again, they would come in every second day. I was always quite good at managing my caseload and this meant that for the majority of the placement, I was able to do hands-on client contact, which is what motivated me. It also meant that I was able to talk to and engage with other professionals and do a lot of co- and interdisciplinary working. I felt valued and that I could contribute. I loved getting involved practically, doing assessments, running groups as well as developing my clinical reasoning through discussion and report writing.

I thought, *When I am qualified, I know that I will be able to do my job competently.*

For that placement, I received a distinction. I would not have been able to excel if I had not been in such a supportive environment, or hadn't had the use of a reader and scribe to assist me in those areas.

*

The way that I sometimes distinguish written text is very visual, and I look for capital letters. If the word is "Waterloo", it's the one with the big "W" and "o". So I don't really read; I look at pictures and shapes of words, but a lot of words look very similar to me because of that.

If I am looking for a word that I anticipate finding, like in a restaurant where you are going to find "chicken" (which is something that I may like) on a menu, or "mushrooms" (which I don't like), I may just scan and look for "m"s and "c"s. I'll then ask someone to read me this or that item (but not this one, because it has "m"s, and I probably won't like it).

When I am using assistive software or trying to open a document, it is again visual. It is where I have placed it; it's the third column from the right, the third from the bottom, with a dot or a symbol. If I am trying to take a note of something, I will often draw a little picture or write the initial of it: the initial is enough of a trigger for me. If I try to scribble down some writing, you won't necessarily be able to understand what it is if you try to make sense of it from a spelling point of view.

When I was learning anatomy, the text-to-voice software didn't really work because the subject consists of a lot of diagrams in the textbook. When the software was reading it to me, it didn't mean anything. Again, it was literally like a foreign language with some words that sounded similar: for example, you have abduction and adduction, ab-duction and ad-duction; you have brachialis and brachoradialis and lots of other words that are very similar. Then there are different muscles and differences in where they insert, and where the origin is, as well as what nerve innervates them. I found an app to help me, which had interactive graphics. It was useful in helping me to practise anatomy prior to anatomy class.

My learning style, as I have said before, is that I have to visualise something, so Colm, who is a physio, drew the muscles onto my arm and colour coordinated them so that all those muscles that were innervated by the same nerve were coloured in a set colour. If the ulnar nerve distribution was blue, then I knew that any of the muscles drawn in blue were innervated by it. It meant that when I did come to do the exam, I could just visualise my arm, and I could see red, blue, and green lines and shapes showing where they did or didn't intersect.

I also made up these little rhymes and stories with another classmate who found anatomy a bit difficult. These helped me visualise the different muscles, so they made sense and interacted, and had some meaning for me, as opposed to just being a list of words to learn.

We had to sit an anatomy exam that covered all of the anatomy that we had learned over the two years. This was a two-and-a-half-hour exam that involved reading and writing. I asked if I could have a scribe and reader for this. I was sanctioned one, but only one who had no anatomy or science background. To me, this seemed strange, because for my Leaving Cert, I always had somebody who understood the (foreign) language, and who was at least familiar with the spelling and pronunciation of specific terminology. This would make sense, as all of my peers who were reading the anatomy exam were also able to read these words and spell them, since we had been studying them for the last two years.

Again, the person who was selected for me was the person who was available. Having a new scribe can be awkward because you are in a very stressful exam situation and don't necessarily know their skillset. You hope that the person is a competent reader and note taker. You also have to sit quite close to them, as oftentimes you are sharing an exam paper, although I always request that, if possible, we be given a copy each. I have a very heightened sense of smell, and I can be distracted if I have to sit beside someone for a long period who has quite a strong odour. I can get fixated on the smell.

For the anatomy exam, I was given a scribe who actually turned up five minutes late for my exam. He had a cup of coffee in his hand, which was fine, except for the fact that he had been late! On top of that, he had no knowledge of anatomy, physiology, or science in general, so when he was trying to read stuff he would say, "Ganeistro … whatever."

And I would ask, "Are you saying *gastrocnemius*?"

"Oh, I don't know," he'd respond. "I think so. Maybe."

It made it very difficult for me to understand what was being asked of me because my reader was somebody trying to read a 'foreign' language. Again, when I started talking about the sagittal plane, he asked me how to spell "plane".

"I don't know," I'd say. "Can you just write sagittal plane?"

169

I also had two staff members in the room with me and had been told the exam would be taped. It was stressful enough having this anatomy exam with a scribe and reader with no knowledge in this area. At least if you write a silly answer down on the paper, it's only the marker who sees it, or you can cross it out afterwards. But I had a live audience of three.

For me to pronounce words, I often have to visualise things. For example, in the middle of the exam I said, "tomato". The scribe began to write down "tomato", and I saw one of the staff members look up at me as I said, "No, no! *Somato*, as in somatosensory. Don't write 'tomato' down: I just have to say *tomato* so that I can then pronounce *somatosensory*."

Sometimes, I get verbal dyspraxia and I find it difficult to say words. Even though I can think about words, I don't know how to start approaching the word. One solution that I have developed over the last few years is to visualise something and say something that associates with it so I can then feel the sound. Otherwise, I find it difficult to coordinate words, especially when I am anxious, with words that I am not familiar with, or names that I cannot quite visualise. I am not able to visualise what "somato" looks like, but I can visualise "tomato", and from that ... somato. That's just one example and a bit of insight into how I work.

*

One of the assignments that I was most looking forward to was a presentation. We were to deliver a case study presentation, using models and research and focusing on intervention.

I thought, *Brilliant! This is something that I am going to excel at because I'm not going to need a scribe, and if I do, certainly not to the extent that I needed one in the past. I am very competent at presenting!*

I compiled my PowerPoint presentation, decided what I was going to say, memorised the dates, facts, and articles, and gave the presentation. Everyone else who presented that day simply read out an essay. Most people stood up and literally read a 2000-word essay that they had written from a sheet while putting some images and quotations on the projector. Others read from little cue cards, but *everybody* got up and read. Nobody got up and just presented.

I felt I was at a disadvantage. It seemed to me that this wasn't a presentation assignment as much as having to write an essay and read it aloud.

I thought, *Well, next time, if there is another assignment like this and I know the actual objective, I will write an essay and then maybe press play on my text-to-voice speech app to get that to read it.* I would have gotten a better grade if I was able to include more facts and quotes but it was not possible to retain that level of information. My classmates barely stopped to breathe when "presenting". They did not "refer" to their notes: it was *readreadreadfactfactfact* rather than an actual presentation with engagement and demonstrations. It felt like a reading competition rather than a *presentation*.

I did okay, but it was not one of my highest grades.

*

The most special piece of paper that I have is my MSc in Occupational Therapy graduation certificate. As a child, and even as an adult, I have been accused of not valuing pieces of paper. They often end up scrunched up or folded in half,

171

scribbled on or torn. But the day I got my degree and walked across the stage was one of the proudest moments of my life. I felt incredibly successful.

I wanted to say to the eight-year-old me, "Look, don't worry. You will achieve. You are smart and you can do it."

In university a student's grades aren't final until they are reviewed by an examination board. For my MSc, I knew I was in the running for a distinction, but wasn't sure if the final result would be a little bit under or a little bit over. I cried when I got my grades with "Mark Awarded: Distinction". Even then, I didn't believe it, because I was afraid that they had made a mistake, and I had to wait until I got the paper in the post. But I got my distinction, and I felt immensely proud. It was validating to get the grade that reflected the amount of energy and time that I had put into the degree. I was delighted, and filled with pride that I could share this experience with my mum and Colm.

When I went back to university, I was very much interested in becoming a Paediatric Occupational Therapist. This was what my background was in, having worked as a youth leader for children and teenagers with disabilities, a swim teacher, a children's camp leader, having run drama and self-advocacy courses for children and adults with disabilities, and for adolescents with social difficulties and dyspraxia. Of course, having had my own difficulties as child, this specialisation made sense.

All through my degree, I would do extracurricular Continuing Professional Development (CPD) courses. I also purchased all of the Paediatric Occupational Therapy books. I was pleased that I did a placement in learning disability and another 10-week placement in a paediatric setting. When we had essay assignments, I gravitated towards paediatrics, in particular developmental coordination disorder and paediatric neurology.

After graduation, people typically say that you should do rotations through various subspecialties. The idea is you shouldn't specialise without having experienced a range of areas. I was adamant that all I wanted to do was be a Paediatric Occupational Therapist. I self-funded the first module of a Sensory Integration Post Graduate course, having put the money aside prior to commencing my degree.

*

I applied for two Paediatric jobs. I interviewed for the first one and the feedback was that I did really well, but I just completely threw away the first question, which was, "*Tell us about your skills and attributes*". I presumed that, as I had already done a written application, that they knew all of those things, so I just mentioned one or two additional things that were not on my CV. They reported afterwards that they could see that I had multiple skills from my CV, but that they could not take this into account and could only go by what I had mentioned in the interview. Needless to say, I didn't get offered the role.

My next interview was for a permanent post in a "Children with Disabilities Team". The first question, again, was, "*Tell us about your skills and attributes.*" This time, I understood the system and answered the question in detail. I often find things easier and less daunting the second time I experience something. So it was no surprise that the second time I had an interview, I would do better and I was offered the job.

*

173

My boss was a *real OT*, as I would say. She was good at problem solving and passionate about enabling people, and it was lovely to work with someone like that, in such a supportive environment. When it came to my having additional needs, difficulties with reading and writing, there was some compensatory strategies that I could use. I had templates and would make a lot of phone calls instead of doing emails all the time. But there were still some written components to my work and elements that software can't read to me; for this, I was sanctioned a few hours a week to pay an administrative support worker to come and support me in my role by helping with reading and writing. My boss sourced an amazing person for this position, who was such a competent reader and typist. She could spell everything and was so unassuming. Honestly, she was like my right hand, and because we worked together for such a long time, we became seamless in our interaction. She understood where I wanted to save things and what way I would set things up. I would drive the mouse; she the keyboard. She also became a friend. I was so successful with my supports that I was able to hold a large caseload and never felt lacking. I stayed in this role until I had my first baby and decided that a move back to Ireland would be best for my family.

I had lots of opportunities to avail of continuing professional development, and a lot of support around that. I got the Elizabeth Casson Award of £1000 to go towards my Sensory Integration modules and work supported me with the time off for study. I found this postgraduate training so interesting. In understanding the neuroanatomical basis of sensory integration difficulties, I gained skills not just for my clients, but for me as a person with sensory processing disorder.

When I was in London, we went out to buy a car we had seen online, but when we got to the dealership, another car caught my eye. I got so excited when I saw a Vauxhall Corsa, the car that I learned to drive in. We changed our plans and ended up buying the Corsa for double the price of the car we had originally planned to purchase. The Corsa just felt familiar. I went on the insurance and did a little bit of driving. When I became pregnant, I found that the challenges of driving became greater. My spatial awareness and balance were more impaired. My pregnancy related tiredness meant that I tended to pass on opportunities to practice driving.

When our first baby was born we decided to leave London and move back to Dublin to be closer to family. Colm and I drove to Holyhead to catch the ferry with our 10 day old baby and our little Corsa filled with all our possessions. Once back in Ireland, I started driving more. I arranged some more lessons, but with a new driving instructor closer to where we were renting. I felt I needed some more structure to prepare for the test and to help me get more organised. Again, he was very firm with me, but I explained how my brain worked and he gave me some visual images as to why the car works the way it does, which was really useful.

The date of my driving test was scheduled for the day that we were due to sign for our new house. I remember thinking, *This is either going to be a brilliant day or a dreadful day.* During the test, I was so anxious that I pulled the car over and said, "I am so sorry, but my leg won't stop shaking. I am going to wait until my leg stops shaking before I drive on." I remember asking myself if that was the right move or not, but I took some deep breaths and then my leg calmed down. Afterwards, the driving tester told me to pull the car over, park it, and get out of the car. I asked him if I'd failed, and he said he could not say anything until we got back to the office, but he asked why I thought I had failed. I said, "Oh, because of my leg." He told me he could not say anything, but he had obviously been inputting things into the iPad while I was driving, so he knew the answer. We went into the office and he sat opposite me and said, "Okay. I just want to let you know that the outcome of today is that you passed your driving test." I burst into tears. All of the pent-up emotion just flowed out of me. When I came downstairs, Colm was waiting. He gave me a hug, thinking that it had not gone well. Only a little while later did I tell him, "I passed!".

I left my 'N' stickers for 'Novice Driver' on the car well beyond the required timeframe. They made me feel a bit safer especially as I was soon to be pregnant again with my 2nd child. It was great being back in Dublin and having family close by, especially as Stuart, and now Killian, had both developed severe health issues.

*

Like Stuart, Killian was also diagnosed with a complex and rare medical condition, and his health got progressively worse over the years. The condition was incurable, and Killian had profound health and care needs. He had been in and out of hospitals over a few years with long hospital stays, some coinciding with Christmas. One year, this resulted in us postponing our family Christmas celebration until January. In July 2019, Killian was admitted to hospital, as his condition was unstable. He had been doing reasonably well, and I dropped by to say "Hi" to him on my way to a family holiday to Belfast. The morning of Colm and my wedding anniversary, Colm had been up with our third child who was almost 4 months old. He popped in to tell me that Mum was on the phone. I took the phone from him and heard my mum tell me that Killian had died. "It's going to be okay," I said. "It's going to be okay." I then burst into tears and couldn't talk. My whole body shook. I had known how sick he was, but he had been extremely unwell before and had managed to recover enough to go home. Despite his long illness, his death was still a shock.

I was not able to get to the hospital quickly enough before he was moved to the undertakers, but I did come to the family home where my other siblings were, and we waited for Killian's body to be returned. Killian had a white coffin lined in pink, which was what he would have picked: totally Killian's taste. My mum had the idea that we would paint and write little messages on the coffin, which seemed a little bit sacrilegious initially, but actually it was a very peaceful thing to do. One of Killian's favourite things to do was to sit at his desk, listen to his music, and draw in his books. He loved when people would sit and colour with him. Friends who came to say goodbye and process the reality that Killian was gone, sat, wrote notes and coloured; it was a calming and reflective process.

Killian had a bright, happy, big personality. And so too was his funeral: it was him to a T. My brother Robert drove me to the church and there was a mile of cars parked on the road up to the church. The amount of people outside and inside the church was enormous. All of these people came to celebrate his life and show support for the family. Everyone wore bright-coloured clothes. During the service, "Mamma Mia", one of Killian's favourites, was played and signed by two lovely interpreters who'd worked with Killian. They were almost dancing on the altar. A couple of butterflies came into the church and kept sitting on the altar. I remember crying and my brother Stuart putting his hand on my shoulder from the pew behind me. There were a lot of unsaid things that were just felt.

At the graveside, my family helped wheel the coffin the last bit. Stuart was in a wheelchair and also on oxygen, but I remember he also stood and helped push Killian to his graveside. I did not want to leave the coffin to be filled in later and just walk away. I had asked Mum if we could fill the grave and we brought a bunch of shovels. Colm, Robert, some of my cousins, and Killian's friends and I filled the grave. It was scorching hot and I remember standing in my bare feet because my shoes were not appropriate for the muddy ground, with a shovel in hand. It was strangely calming doing such labour-intensive work at a time of extreme grief.

Like Killian, Stuart's complex health issues got progressively worse. His rare disorder was causing multiple organ issues. His lungs were under a lot of pressure and he was a full-time oxygen user. He also needed dialysis several times a week. In March 2020, when Covid hit, it was very worrying, as he had to go in and out of hospital regularly and he would've been in the most high-risk category if he caught the virus. He had gone in for his regular dialysis appointment, and again they didn't like his oxygen levels, so they kept him in. They tested him for Covid and he was all clear, but he was still very sick. I was seven months pregnant with my fourth child and couldn't visit him in the hospital. A Zoom call was arranged, and my mum and siblings were on it, and we told our favourite stories of Stuart, talking about our childhood, and Robert played guitar. That night, I spoke with him on the phone. I said everything I needed to say, but hoped there was no need to say anything. He had a good next day. But Mum called a few hours later to say Stuart had just passed away. Again, my body went into shock, but this time I was trying hard to calm down as I knew it could be bad for the baby in my tummy. The double loss in less than nine months made it all feel greater. Stuart's funeral was a complete contrast to Killian's. I didn't sit for hours at his coffin surrounded by family and friends. Instead, it was a short visit on my own. The crematorium was limited to 10 people in total: just parents, siblings, his wife, and her family. There was also a five-kilometre travel restriction in place, but I'm pretty sure I saw a few of Stuart's friends from further afield standing at the gates. It was awful. It didn't feel real: no hugs, no celebration of his life.

Both Stuart and Killian were fighters, and I am so grateful to have had them as my brothers.

*

During the height of Covid (before any sign of vaccinations and in the midst of hard lockdowns) I had a four-year-old, a three-year-old, a one-year-old, and a six weeks-old baby. Colm suffered a back injury and ended up with really bad sciatica. I was breastfeeding our new-born at the time, and had no help because of the risks of Covid and high case numbers. It was horrific. Colm couldn't sleep or sit up, and had to eat lying in a very particular position. I went to pick up medication for Colm, and was trying to dart back to the kids when my new smartphone fell out of my pocket. As I closed the door, it got caught and broke in half; the screen was smashed and I could not use my phone. I got home and just started crying, and my little boy said, "Mommy, are you sad because your brothers are dead?" I just kept crying. I remember thinking that I couldn't cope; and then I realised that I had to cope. Who else was going to mind all of my babies? Just like that, a switch went off and I got up and started doing what needed doing. I had to take it day by day, and yes, it was a rubbish time. One of my ways of coping was that I would just laugh about it and remind myself, *This too shall pass.*

Luckily for both of us, it was not a long-term thing; Colm's back improved eventually, there was a bigger stretch between feeds and I was not as sleep deprived.

It definitely made me realise that, yes, just because some bad things happen does not mean that worse things can't happen. Equally, life is transient, and you need to keep facing challenges, and you need to factor in self-care, too. This is something that is so key for everyone, but especially for parents. Whether it is a walk, a bath, doing a hobby, watching telly, writing in a diary, it is vital. For me, self-care takes the form of swimming in the sea. Swimming in the sea was probably what kept me going at the height of the pandemic, and it definitely helped with my bereavements.

I did not have an opportunity to grieve for my brothers, because I couldn't. Life was busy and I had my own babies to mind. I was in the moment, getting by, day by day. But as it was nearing the first year of my brother Stuart's anniversary, I wanted to get some bereavement counselling. It was done virtually. I struggled even initially to find time to do those one-hour weekly sessions over six weeks. That made me realise that if I could not even take an hour out of my week for myself, then I was not prioritising my self-care or teaching my kids self-care. The bereavement counselling was not what I expected it to be. It required me to do a lot of reflection and sitting with emotions. I finished my sessions and realised that if I took an hour each week, the world would not stop turning and my family would cope. So I made it a habit to just do something really positive for myself for an hour a week. It actually made me a much better parent, and probably a better partner. Life will throw us challenges. The more we dig, and the more we go out into the world, the more challenges we will find. But we *can* solve these problems; we *can* change things. It is not always exactly how we want it to be, but it is good enough.

A Crossroads

Afterword

Luck helps the brave.

My book naturally finished when I stopped dictating it in 2014. But I didn't feel I could leave out the fact my brothers had passed away, as they were key characters in my story and such significant people in my life. I found the process of writing this memoir quite emotionally draining, as I was reliving my life events. It is odd to see one's life written out in sequence. To me, it plays like a movie, which allows me to remove myself and consider how others may perceive these events. I visualise a little girl, a little *me*, and I feel so protective of her. Then, as she becomes a teenager, I see a girl to whom I want to say, *Shh, don't say, don't do that,* and I cringe, but I also see an innocence and honesty that is beautiful. I wouldn't be so passionate about helping others and righting wrongs if I hadn't experienced these struggles, or if I was neuro-typical. I now embrace being neuro-diverse. It is absolutely fine that I see things differently.

The stories I've shared, and the many more that were left untold, have all contributed to who I am today. I would not have achieved what I did without the significant people in my life. I feel privileged to have my mum as my mother. They say you only need one adult to believe in you, and I always had that. I have become so good at making friends, but more importantly, at keeping them. I love being an Occupational Therapist, and I see ways of removing obstacles for others. I am particularly skilled at this because I have years of practice of having to do this for myself!

I once dictated a letter and sent it to the teachers in my secondary school. I asked them to consider stopping an award system in the school which was divided into "daytime" and "night-time" awards. The "night-time" awards (or higher-tier awards, as

I called them) were presented during an evening event, where parents were invited and refreshments were provided. These were for students who had the top grades, who fitted the academic mould. The "daytime" awards were for students who tried hard, and were generally given to those with disabilities or where there were difficulties at home. I pointed out that it was easy for students to do well when they had no additional challenges, food on the table, educated parents, and funds for extra tuition. The system was not equitable.

To this day, societal systems are not equitable. In life, we are often not measuring ourselves up against reality. We are often not comparing like with like. I think it is important that we stop suggesting that life is shiny and easy. We are all different and that's okay.

Sometimes I forget I have my disabilities. When barriers are removed and systems work effectively, I think that I can read and write. It is only when I independently try and read or write that I am surprised at the realisation. I have upskilled and achieved so much academically and professionally, but my reading and writing ability has not improved. I see my children meeting their developmental milestones and breezing through life. I see qualities in them that are reflective of the best in me. Sometimes my eldest son brings home his Senior Infants homework, and I am unsure what the instructions are asking us to do. We both read the directions and I decide we'll wait for Colm to come home to explain that particular exercise. The realisation has dawned on me that my son is almost at the same reading age as me.

A key motivator for me in writing my book was to shed light on these difficulties, so that people might gain a better understanding of what it is like to have hidden disabilities. Not much is known about dyspraxia and its impact on other areas beyond motor planning. My life story illustrates my understanding of how this condition has affected me. I have mixed feelings about sharing my stories. I know I am leaving myself open to criticism and the cruel reality of being in the public eye. But there is a need to generate more understanding of the lived experience. I tried to avoid writing this memoir from the point of view of a clinician. Although professional opinions are certainly of value, there is a need to give a voice to the individuals who experience disability. The pendulum can swing from one side of the spectrum to the other, from the professional to the lived experience. I believe that striking a balance between the two yields the best results. I am keen for the reader to interpret what they want from my life stories and take from them what they need. I hope my memoir helps people know that they are not alone in their struggles. I hope it is useful to read how my struggles played out.

I am happy to say that access in public libraries has improved significantly. Now, I can download free audiobooks on the Borrowbox app. Paid apps such as Audible are also excellent, with books narrated by amazing readers. Many of my non-dyslexic friends use these apps to listen to audiobooks, as they find the experience enjoyable. Technology has continued to improve and open more doors, but one downside is the current tendency for children to share embarrassing video content of their peers. I can only imagine that I would have been an easy target with all my rejections and embarrassing events – I had so many! I learnt to navigate challenging social systems before the advent of mobile phones. When I was 14, I once used the landline to phone a boy in the year above me and tell him directly that I liked him. In the background, I could hear other people sniggering. His sister and her friend had been listening in on the other line and heard the whole conversation ... Awkward! But I didn't let this experience stop me. If I had stopped being true to myself, I might never have asked Colm out for a coffee, and I wouldn't have had my wonderful children and been happily married for more than a decade. So fortune favours, or luck helps, as Luigi once said, the brave!

I am still known for being direct, but now this is considered one of my strengths. As a child, we are taught to hold our tongue; we learn to conform, sit still, think like others, and behave in a way that fits the mould. I could never do this. We do need to learn to get along and work together towards common goals. Adults often admire the honesty and directness of children, and yet we continue to project a need to conform onto the next generation. I still continue to put myself out there and have new experiences. I keep learning, and I continue to grow into myself. Occasionally, I will get caught in that trap of holding myself up against other people's values. It's like a wave that grabs you when you are swimming in the sea. You need to put your feet down and say, "No, I'm going this way. These are my values."

Ironically, I have a tendency to write letters about things that I feel should change. When I was 12, I dictated one of these letters when I realised that Killian was to communicate using sign language. I wanted everyone to be able to communicate with

187

him. I decided that if we all learnt to sign in school and we had sign language as an official language, then no one who was deaf would be left out of society. I sent this letter to all the Government minsters and the President at the time. I got several replies in white envelopes with the state emblem of a gold harp embossed on the outside, saying it was a lovely idea and that they would consider it. The idea that all children could learn sign language in school is based on the same inclusive concepts I still believe in today. If society can work to remove barriers and make things accessible to all, no one will be marginalised.

Growing up, I often felt like I didn't belong and couldn't fit in. My journey has led me to realise that I do belong, that I do have a place. I like to use the analogy of a child's shape sorter, with different shapes and spaces. Most people may be circles, but I am a triangle; if you try to shove a triangle through a circular opening, it doesn't work. Maybe if you insist and shove it, force it enough, eventually it will get through, but ultimately it is likely to be a broken, fragile interpretation of a circle. But if you take the time to turn the shape sorter and understand, to find the triangular space, you can pass it through and have a happy shape, still intact and unbroken among all the other shapes. I really believe there is a space for everyone!

I am Hannah. I am not wrong, and I am not broken.
I'm just different.

\- *Hannah Daly*

Acknowledgements

Acknowledgements

I would like to thank all those involved in making this book possible. To Colm, my wonderful husband, for always believing in, and supporting me. Without you, the book may never have been realised. To my mum, for being my mum and helping me get to where I am today. To my siblings and all in the book who contributed positively to my journey. To Gill Morrey for typing up my stories without question and for doing the final proof read. To Rachel O' Kelly for an amazing cover design. To Lois Edmonds for being my first reader of a draft manuscript. To Sarah Dron, Michelle Kelly, and Jen Ryan, thank you for doing in-depth readings and offering editing suggestions. To Shoumen and Rebecca for your support. To Ger Kenny for his support in bringing this book to fruition and telling me this project was worth doing. To Harry Conway for his positivity and support. To Claire Strombeck for the developmental and copy edits. To Ronan Lupton SC for his support and advice. To Karen Power for guiding me on self-publishing. To Alan Heary at Print Dynamics. To Conor Horgan for his talent and support. To Sean Walsh at Millbrook Studios for his honesty and unbelievable generosity in helping me achieve the audiobook. To Clare McKenna for reading the audiobook. To Barry McCall, Eoghan Brennan, Arthur Carron and Christophe Majani d'Inguimbert for giving me permission to use their photos. To all my test readers and supporters, Joey, Samantha, Rhona, Helen, Kate, Aoife, Sarah, Deirdre, Rachel, Ken, Joanna and all those who believed in and supported the book Finally to my children, to whom the future belongs, for making me want to make the world a better place.

Printed in Great Britain
by Amazon

22759217R00111